W9-DDJ-284

BrainSMART®
Teacher Leadership:
Stories, Strategies, and Celebrations
Third Edition

Donna Wilson
and Marcus Conyers

BrainSMART Teacher Leadership: Stories, Strategies, and Celebrations
ISBN number 1-58933-154-0
Authors Donna Wilson and Marcus Conyers
Publication Date 2009
Orlando, Florida: BrainSMART

Copyright © 2009 by BrainSMART® Inc. All rights reserved. No part of this publication may be reproduced or transmitted in any form or by any means, electronic or mechanical, including photocopy, recording, or any other information storage and retrieval system without permission from BrainSMART. For permission to reproduce any part of this material, contact BrainSMART. Phone: (407) SMART61. Fax: (800) 725-5508. Web site: http://www.brainsmart.com.

BrainSMART is a registered trademark.

BrainSMART Authors, Instructional Designers, and Program Developers: Donna Wilson and Marcus Conyers

Dedication

Dr. Wells Singleton (left), Provost, Fischler School of Education and Human Services at Nova Southeastern University, with BrainSMART founders Donna Wilson and Marcus Conyers

This book is dedicated to the leaders who truly inspire us. First, to Dr. Wells Singleton, Provost, Fischler School of Education and Human Services, who gave us the opportunity to co-develop possibly the world's first distance graduate programs in brain-based education so that any classroom teacher could learn to teach in ways the brain may learn best. We look forward to our brainstorming meetings with him more than any other! Also, we would like to recognize the hundreds of teacher leaders who are positively transforming the lives of their students and colleagues.

Our thanks also go to Dr. Denise Kelly, program director, for all of her assistance from 1999 onward and for everything she does so these programs flourish each term! Thanks also go to the faculty who understand how important it is to support teacher leaders today with passion, current knowledge, and necessary skills.

Lastly, we want to thank our team members, Mary Collington and Mary Buday, the best 'brains on the plane' who lead brilliantly in their unique areas.

BrainSMART
Teacher Leadership:
Stories, Strategies, and Celebrations

Contents

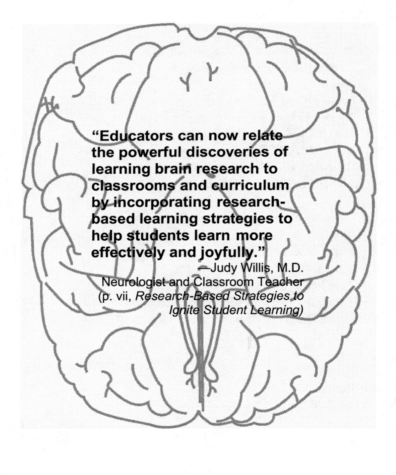

"Educators can now relate the powerful discoveries of learning brain research to classrooms and curriculum by incorporating research-based learning strategies to help students learn more effectively and joyfully."

—Judy Willis, M.D.
Neurologist and Classroom Teacher
(p. vii, *Research-Based Strategies to Ignite Student Learning*)

BrainSMART
Teacher Leadership:
Stories, Strategies, and Celebrations

Contents

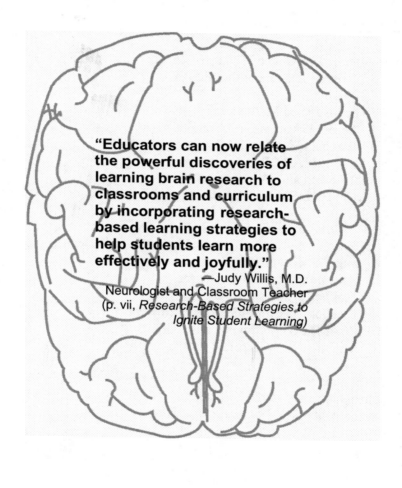

"Educators can now relate the powerful discoveries of learning brain research to classrooms and curriculum by incorporating research-based learning strategies to help students learn more effectively and joyfully."

—Judy Willis, M.D.
Neurologist and Classroom Teacher
(p. vii, *Research-Based Strategies to Ignite Student Learning*)

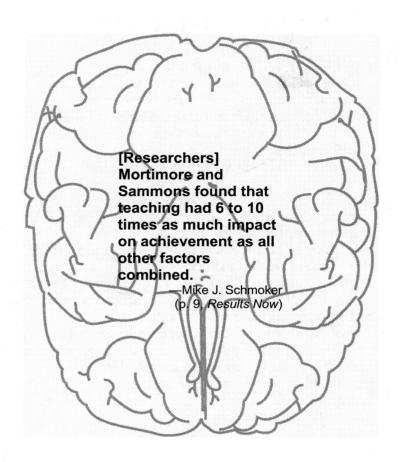

[Researchers] Mortimore and Sammons found that teaching had 6 to 10 times as much impact on achievement as all other factors combined.

—Mike J. Schmoker
(p. 9, *Results Now*)

Introduction:
In Praise of Teacher Leaders

Within every school there is a sleeping giant of teacher leadership which can be a strong catalyst for making change. By using the energy of teacher leaders as agents for school change the reform of public education will stand a better chance of building momentum.
—Marilyn Katzenmeyer & Gayle Moller, 2001

BrainSMART teacher leadership integrates theories and research on teacher leadership with the BrainSMART approach to effective instruction.
—Marcus Conyers & Donna Wilson

This book is in praise of the thousands of teacher leaders we have been privileged to meet through our graduate studies and professional development over the last ten years. These educators are making an extraordinary difference in the lives of their students and colleagues. We have benefited a great deal by learning with them, and we want to share some of their stories here.

Our goal in this text is to affirm the importance of teacher leaders and to illustrate how universally these brain-based methods work in support of teacher leaders. Of course, just as each brain is different, so is each teacher story and interview.

There are various approaches to instruction. This book shines the spotlight on teachers who have studied brain-based methods with us over the last decade. A central tenet of the BrainSMART approach is that as a teacher leader, you hold a key to the future in your hands.

Our hearts are often touched as we hear teachers share their stories about classroom successes. From the Atlantic seaboard to the Pacific, from the U.S. northern border to the south, educators are teaching students how to be more effective learners of important subject matter knowledge. Often, when these teachers share their stories, we also hear their passion for teaching. It seems that the success they are experiencing rekindles the early enthusiasm they brought with them into the profession.

These educators are making an extraordinary difference in the lives of their students and colleagues.

A middle-aged teacher told us, "I came into teaching to reach students who have trouble learning, and with new methods, I do! After a number of years, before learning new strategies, I was pretty burned out. Now, I'm glad to be teaching once again!"

Another teacher, fresh from her university undergraduate teaching program, said, "Wow! I had heard a little bit about the brain in school, but now I have lots of practical strategies to use when I teach. We are delighted this program is so usable in the classroom and in life at home with my children."

For more than two decades Marcus and I have been teaching teachers cognitive and brain-based approaches to increase student achievement. Through professional development in schools and now for almost a decade through Nova Southeastern University's (NSU) Fischler School of Education and Human Services, we have been working to provide cutting-edge graduate studies in brain-based teaching to students. We are very proud of these graduate studies with NSU, because this gives teachers a chance to learn practical instructional tools and earn a graduate degree at the same time. Further, most would agree that professional learning is most

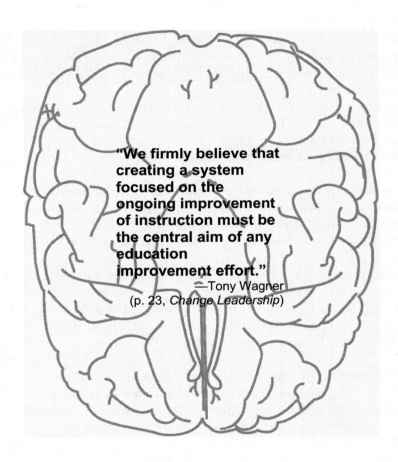

"We firmly believe that creating a system focused on the ongoing improvement of instruction must be the central aim of any education improvement effort."
—Tony Wagner
(p. 23, *Change Leadership*)

powerful over an extended period of time, with the opportunity to apply what is learned in the classroom. Often, we meet teacher leaders when we are invited into schools, districts, and communities to present, or we hear from them through e-mail. What we're hearing from these teacher leaders causes us to believe that many of these teachers now graduating from our NSU graduate studies have the passion, will, knowledge, and skills to positively transform schools across this country.

Few would argue that teachers are the most important professionals in the educational community. Furthermore, it is now known that instruction is the aspect of education that best predicts student success or failure.

While instruction—more than policy, curriculum, or student characteristics—is the best predictor of whether students will succeed in school, it is important that students be taught how to be effective thinkers. The abilities to think well and to use metacognition are the most important student characteristics needed for academic success today.

Teacher Leaders in the 'Real World'

It occurred to us that a good way to learn how teacher leaders are using their graduate studies in the "real world" of school and even at home with their families would be for someone to ask them. We hired a journalist and an editor to do some interviews with graduates who had touched base with us about how the linkages

> The purpose of this little book is to illuminate the practice of teacher leaders who have learned key research about their chosen profession and want to share it with others.

between our content and their lives of teaching and learning. In some cases those interviews appear verbatim and in others as short feature stories.

This book, written in praise of teacher leaders, has as its focus stories, interviews, and comments from brain-based graduate

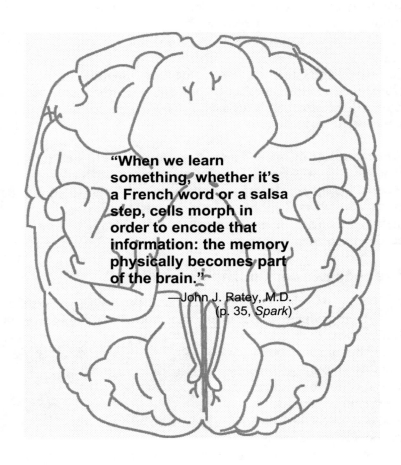

"When we learn something, whether it's a French word or a salsa step, cells morph in order to encode that information: the memory physically becomes part of the brain."

—John J. Ratey, M.D.
(p. 35, *Spark*)

program students who are attending NSU now or have graduated from these programs within the past seven years. There are also two grant projects successfully used to apply for funding for technology or materials for classrooms, as well as a classroom research project using brain-based teaching. Our hope is that as you read these stories and interviews where teachers talk about the strategies they have used, you will feel camaraderie with some of these teachers. As teacher leaders, maybe you will even be further encouraged to share some of the strategies with teachers at your school site.

Teaching is often an isolated profession, especially if teachers choose the road of change in their lives as a result of their lifelong learning. The purpose of this little book is to illuminate the practice of teacher leaders who have learned key research about their chosen profession and want to share it with others. We feel strongly that by sharing teacher leaders' stories, momentum is building for more teachers to experience the joy that comes from a life of teaching rather than experiencing the burnout naturally associated with more paperwork, political accountability, and even a lack of respect in some communities.

Instruction Is Key

Often missing from the teacher leadership literature are important elements of positive instruction, the *how*. I am speaking of the missing element as the science. Often, I have read or heard seemingly miraculous teacher stories by individual teachers. I have often experienced the power of the story but felt that there wasn't anything that I could take away to become a better educator myself or a replicable strategy I could take to share with other teachers. The interviews and stories we share from teacher leaders across the country show

> Often missing from the teacher leadership literature are important elements of positive instruction, the *how—the science*.

that when graduate study in education is based on research distilled into practical structures and strategies for teaching, teachers apply their studies to the classroom and love it!

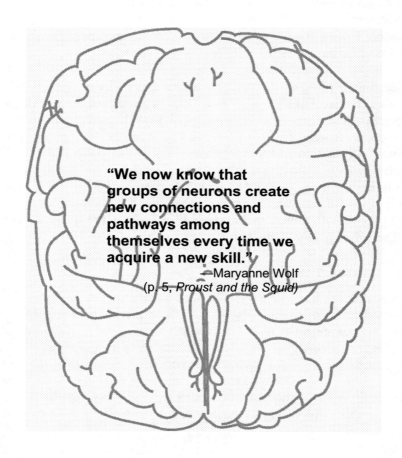

"We now know that groups of neurons create new connections and pathways among themselves every time we acquire a new skill."
—Maryanne Wolf
(p. 5, *Proust and the Squid*)

Brain-Based Methodology:
Across Locations and Content Areas

As a matter of fact, preschool, elementary, middle, and secondary

Susan Hyzer, teacher of gifted students, with Dr. Wilson

teachers alike across many content areas have used instructional strategies to reach a wide-ranging group of young people. Through Leslie Wilson's eyes, as she taught Head Start and elementary school in small town Oklahoma, I learned that some of the cognitive assets taught in Thinking for Results™ are best used to teach character. Through assets like finishing power and appropriate courage, students can learn to be hard workers and to risk learning, even when it might be publicly difficult.

Susan Hyzer, teacher of intermediate-aged gifted students in suburban Gwinnett County, Georgia, teaches us that the strategies in the text, *BrainSMART 60 Strategies for Boosting Test Scores*, are a great way to capture student interest and help them maximize their learning potential. By the way, as teacher leader, Ms. Hyzer has shared information about her program with hundreds of teachers, thus giving them the opportunity to share in her journey of learning. She now has a number of "generations" of BrainSMART teachers in the elementary school

> Teacher leaders across the United States are changing students' lives for the better through these brain-based instructional methods.

where she enjoys teaching. Teacher leader Heather Toner, an ESL teacher and one of Ms. Hyzer's colleagues in Gwinnett County, recently spoke with me about presenting her research on the cognitive assets necessary for high school students at her professional association's state meeting. Her presentation should be helpful to colleagues, and excerpts are included later in this text.

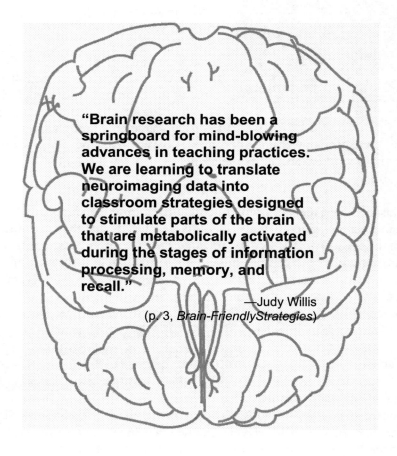

"Brain research has been a springboard for mind-blowing advances in teaching practices. We are learning to translate neuroimaging data into classroom strategies designed to stimulate parts of the brain that are metabolically activated during the stages of information processing, memory, and recall."

—Judy Willis
(p. 3, *Brain-Friendly Strategies*)

Phil Durr, a middle school teacher in Onslow County, North Carolina, attended two weeks of professional development because it was required, and left feeling that he had found some strategies he wanted to try to use in the classroom. Mr. Durr told me he came to the session experiencing some burnout after many years of teaching and working in administration. The story of his current enjoyment of teaching and student response to his changes, as well as his current leadership as teacher, is reported later in this book.

It was in listening to Cherese Copeland in Ft. Wayne, Indiana, that we learned the effect of brain-based movement strategies on the motivation of a pregnant teacher! Mrs. Copeland told us that as she taught third-grade students the strategies to help them learn math facts and saw them learning, she experienced more energy than she had teaching before she was pregnant. We were impressed!

Steve Hawes, an elementary teacher in the Florida Keys, shared that he saw a remarkable gain in learning and test scores when he started using some new cognitive strategies in his classroom. Specifically, Mr. Hawes was excited that the district had targeted math increases as a goal, and his students' math scores went up as a result of use of the instructional strategies.

Teachers Honored by Peers

Congratulations to Leanne Maule, 2009 Georgia Teacher of the Year and student in NSU's Ed.S. program focusing on Brain-Based Education. We congratulate Leanne Maule for her achievement in becoming the teacher of the year in her state. We are impressed with her commitment to creating a classroom designed with brain-based research in mind and for teaching her students practical strategies for enhancing their academic success. Leanne says it best in her brochure:

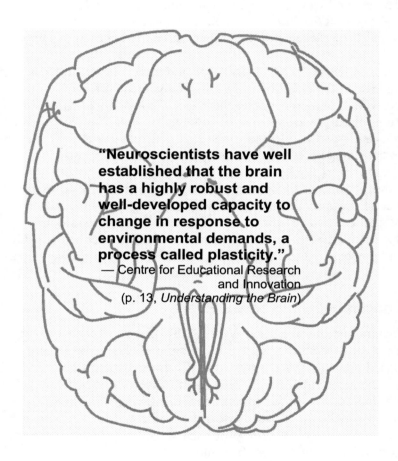

"Neuroscientists have well established that the brain has a highly robust and well-developed capacity to change in response to environmental demands, a process called plasticity."
— Centre for Educational Research and Innovation
(p. 13, *Understanding the Brain*)

Finally! Teachers now have concrete, research-based strategies for improving student performance. Designing the curriculum for all learners with brain-based research in mind is essential for every student's opportunity for personal achievement. I only wish my teachers had known what I know now!

In Texas, Florida, and Georgia, we know of at least six teacher leaders who, like Leanne, have been chosen teacher of the year at the local, county, or state levels across various content domains and from elementary to high school. In these cases, they each speak of their particular stories of teaching and the power of brain-based strategies learned in their graduate studies to shape their teaching in domains across reading, language arts, math, science, ESL, and physical education. From one teacher of the year at the completion of the master's program came this message: "Thank you so much for introducing BrainSMART into my life. I am going for the Specialist's (EdS), starting this month on the 28th. By the way I am Teacher of the Year 2005 for my brand new school. Thanks for offering such a great program where I can grow and make my classroom the best in the school."

BrainSMART Principals

Principal Karen Sinclair in Winter Park, Florida, has graduated from the program and is using what she has learned to support teachers in her school with more strategies to boost learning at the preschool level. Recently, we had a double benefit of Mrs. Sinclair's leading and learning, when team member Mary Buday visited for a multiple day meeting, and her three-year-old daughter, Ella, attended Mrs. Sinclair's school and loved it. (Ella was also delighted that Marcus met her and Mary each day and carried her lunch, and Mary Collington met her daily after school!)

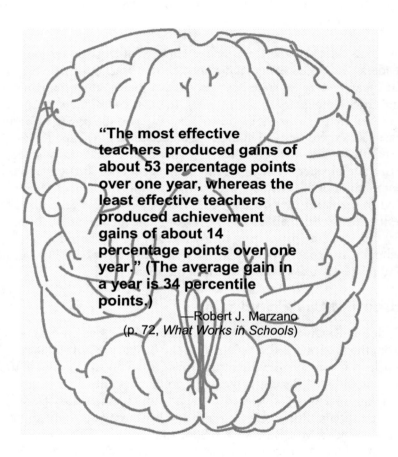

"The most effective teachers produced gains of about 53 percentage points over one year, whereas the least effective teachers produced achievement gains of about 14 percentage points over one year." (The average gain in a year is 34 percentile points.)

—Robert J. Marzano
(p. 72, *What Works in Schools*)

After attending a workshop, Chic Hanson, a principal in New Jersey, has encouraged teachers at his school to infuse BrainSMART strategies into their classroom instructional routines each day. He is very supportive of their efforts and is always curious to learn more strategies to support them.

Research and Community Meet: The BrainSMART Community of Educators

Cognitive and student achievement research now forms the basis for effective instruction. This research is informed by a growing body of literature on brain research that can be applied in the classroom. This research on the brain confirms much of what I studied years ago in cognitive psychology and education. In addition, we now have methods that teachers are using to accelerate instruction while reaching a growing number of diverse learners. A large and growing body of research underpins what we teach. But this is not just about the science of teaching. To Marcus and myself, many of the educators

Mary Collington, Mary Buday with daughter Ella, and Dr. Wilson at a BrainSMART working retreat in Winter Park, Florida

who have learned with us feel like family! As I meet some of you and hear from others, we also know that most of you have one or more friends in the programs. Currently in some counties, more than 100 teachers are in the programs or have graduated.

Priscilla Bourgeois

Graduate student Priscilla Bourgeois, principal from the New Orleans area, says the Ed.S. is what every teacher and administrator need to be effective instructional leaders today. She even went far beyond just talking about BrainSMART

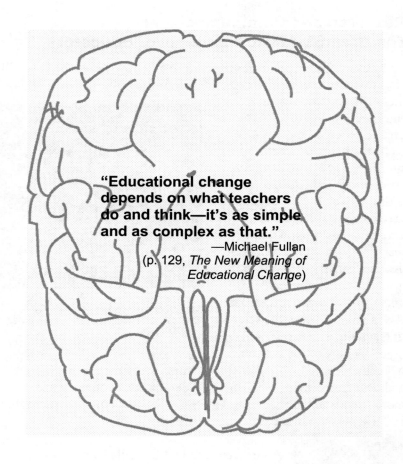

"Educational change depends on what teachers do and think—it's as simple and as complex as that."
—Michael Fullan
(p. 129, *The New Meaning of Educational Change*)

and helped a cadre of her teachers receive a business grant to help pay for their studies so they could be even more effective teachers! Mrs. Bourgeois was one of the first cohort of graduate students who joined NSU in 2001 and began her studies in 2002.

In cohort 2, two teachers at Mrs. Bourgeois's school joined the Master's program, Margie Keyes and Kay Bankston. Already teacher leaders when they came into the program, they learned more new strategies to use in the classroom. They used many strategies from the program and shared tips for healthy learning through healthy eating and exercise habits with parents as well. Mrs. Keyes wrote us that "The kids love the brain foods, and BrainObics. I also include a brain fact on each week's homework sheet. They are becoming very well versed in the topic!" She found joy in teaching even when the final years of her life were not easy. "Our Margie" taught the methods as she fought a brave battle against cancer. These words are a lasting memorial to her teaching.

Just as I will forever remember Margie, I will always smile when I recall hearing Ellen Hooper describe her life circumstances as she was earning the Ed.S. I heard her story when Ellen and Dewey Hooper hosted an NSU facilitation in Savannah, Georgia. During the session, a teacher asked if Mrs. Hooper had found that she could do the Ed.S. in 14 months while working full-time. Ellen smiled broadly and responded, "My grown son, my David, was deployed for Iraq during this period, and I was put on bed rest during the end of my term carrying Julia [the Hoopers' alert baby girl on Ellen's hip]. It was a very stressful time, but we did it!"

Ellen and Dewey Hooper, with daughter Julia, and Dr. Wilson at a live BrainSMART NSU event recruiting new students

Ellen went on to share the many things she had taken from the program and why she likes sharing the information with other teachers so they can

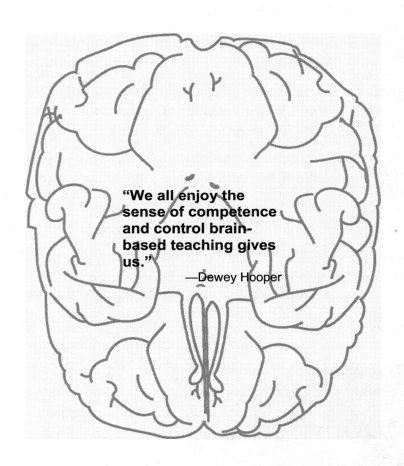

"We all enjoy the sense of competence and control brain-based teaching gives us."

—Dewey Hooper

consider coming into the graduate studies if the time is right for them. Dewey added, "Between my wife and myself, we have several family members who have joined the program, as well as coworkers. We all enjoy the sense of competence and control brain-based teaching gives us." You will hear more from the Hoopers later in this text.

References

Centre for Educational Research and Innovation. (2007). *Understanding the brain: The birth of a learning science.* Danvers, MA: Organisation for Economic Cooperation and Development.

Fullan, M. (2007). *The new meaning of educational change.* New York: Teachers College Press.

Katzenmeyer, M., & Moller, G. (2001). *Awakening the sleeping giant: Helping teachers develop as leaders.* Thousand Oaks, CA: Corwin Press.

Marzano, R. J. (2003). *What works in schools: Translating research into action.* Alexandria, VA: Association for Supervision and Curriculum Development.

Ratey, J. J. (2008). *Spark: The revolutionary new science of exercise and the brain.* New York: Little, Brown.

Schmoker, M. J. (2006). *Results now: How we can achieve unprecedented improvements in teaching and learning.* Alexandria, VA: Association for Supervision and Curriculum Development.

Wagner, T. (2006) *Change leadership: A practical guide to transforming our schools.* San Francisco: Jossey-Bass.

Willis, J. (2006). *Research-based strategies to ignite student learning.* Alexandria, VA: Association for Supervision and Curriculum Development.

Willis, J. (2007). *Brain-friendly strategies for the inclusion classroom.* Alexandria, VA: Association for Supervision and Curriculum Development.

Wolf, M. (2007). *Proust and the squid: The story and science of the reading brain.* New York: HarperCollins.

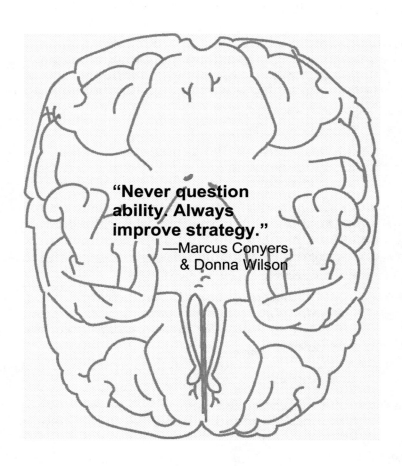

"**Never question ability. Always improve strategy.**"
—Marcus Conyers & Donna Wilson

BrainSMART Teacher Leaders: In Their Own Words

We want to share the following stories of Master's and Educational Specialist students and graduates. Some of these interviews and stories were collected awhile back, and others were told more recently. Many were told because I felt after hearing from them that they had a story about teaching and learning they wanted to tell. Some of the stories have appeared in newsletters and others in local newspapers. Our purpose for compiling the stories and interviews here reflects the spirit of the teachers' decision to tell their stories in the first place—we share their desire to inspire other teachers. And, yes, we want to stand and say we are glad there is such an option for graduate studies in our field.

When I started in education as my chosen profession many years ago, I found that as a teacher, I was isolated. I worked with some great folks. However, with my learning style and background, I wanted to learn the very essence—the core and foundation—of what other teachers were doing so their students could learn effectively. I was always looking for ways to improve my own teaching.

In fact, some of the real students I was teaching didn't fit the profile of my academic study at the university. Furthermore, I didn't feel that I was a part of the mainstream of our profession as I quickly developed a profound interest in reaching students for whom learning didn't come easily. Personally, if I would have had the opportunity, I would have found meeting these teacher leaders through their stories very enriching—as I do today whenever we have that privilege.

— Donna Wilson.

Interviews with Teacher Leaders: Master's Degree

Benjamin Schmauss
Earned: NSU M.S. in BrainSMART Teaching
"The teacher leader concept is a great life principle. I believe in the mantra that goes along with that, that there's spirituality to teaching, a responsibility to give and in giving, we receive."

1. What grade level do you teach, how long have you been teaching, and what is the name of your school?
I teach K–5th grade in Las Vegas, which is the Clark County Public School System. I've been teaching for two years and in June 2007 will complete my Master of Education degree with a focus on BrainSMART.

2. Has the content been useful to you in your work as a classroom teacher?
Absolutely. It's helped me to reach my students in a differentiated way instead of teaching them in the way that I have learned in the past.

For example, using the H.E.A.R. strategy has been helpful. It is a retention/attention strategy where students halt, engage their minds and actively recall information. It gets the kids active in the learning process. I've also enjoyed watching kids benefit from peer partners. Peer partners allow students to articulate information they hear from me to a partner and increase their retention of the information.

I also enjoy some of the classroom management techniques, including the centrally important teacher-student relationship, coaching for thinking, and all of the cognitive strategies, I love them all. Practical optimism helps kids to develop the life skill of enduring and looking at situations in a constructive manner, and allowing them to frame failure as another step to learning and achievement is invaluable.

3. What do you like about earning your degree 100% online?
It's been extremely convenient. I'm a fairly new teacher and a brand new dad of a four-month-old baby. I can give you a list of things I've done this year and I could not have undertaken this program unless it was online. I actually learn, I don't just go through the motions. And very little time is taken away from my family.

4. How does this degree compare with other higher education programs you have studied?
Of all of the other things I've been engaged in, this has had instant application and I enjoy that. It is not just getting the master's to get a pay raise. It is a perk that I am getting tools to improve my trade and improve myself. I feel good about having new skills that improve my effectiveness and competence.

5. Would you recommend this program to other teachers?
Yes, I already have. I have a church friend starting the program in about a month. I think Dr. Donna should consider that I would be a good mentor in the program. I believe in the precepts that they teach and it has the opportunity to really expand in our district. There is a lot of opportunity to implement the teaching strategies in this program.

6. What would you say to other teachers about the program?
One of many teachers' main concerns is family and that usually comes first. This program has the potential to help deliver many things that will improve your life and your career: the cost of the program and the time commitment required to complete the program are both reasonable. The material can be immediately implemented and having gained this educational credential, a teacher can usually count on an increase in compensation. I advanced my career while still meeting all my family's needs.

7. What would you say to an administrator about the program?
Administrators should be focused on meeting teachers' needs and enhancing morale in the school for the benefit of our students. This program meets teachers' needs and gives immediate tools to turn our classrooms into stimulating learning labs where children are engaged and energized. It is challenging and motivating and makes you want to teach in a way students can learn. Teacher leaders leave this program with a great desire to contribute to the overall learning culture of one's school. A lot of the assignments we have are geared toward that. I am creating a program to help teachers increase their students' peer to peer positive interaction and help students feel comfortable taking chances and going outside norms. This program helps create teacher-leaders who feel they actually have something substantive to offer to their peers.

8. What would you say to parents?
One of the greatest things any program does is prevent teacher burnout, and a true teacher is always learning. This program provides students with a teacher who is excited and provides differentiated instruction.

9. What have you enjoyed the most about the content?
The teacher leader concept is a great life principle. I believe in the mantra that goes along with that, that there's spirituality to teaching, a responsibility to give and in giving, we receive. I enjoy that about the program. It has covered a lot of different areas of teaching and has given me something real. The brain research and data about learning, I enjoy the idea they incorporate the whole body. The mind-body-spirit connection tells us that if our nutrition or emotional environment in the classroom, or even our physical education is not in sync, if we don't get kids moving in our classrooms, they will continue to have a lower level of education in comparison to different cultures and nations.

10. Did you have a friend or colleague who took the program? What did they say about the program?
One friend is just signing up. I've had numerous colleagues

approach me with questions about the program. I try to promote that new teachers can get in and get going with this, you can get all of this done in 14 months, with so many more skills and within three years the increase in pay will cover the initial investment in tuition. It's well worth it for teachers.

Tammy Daugherty
Earned: NSU M.S. in BrainSMART Teaching; working toward Ed.S. degree
"I like to talk shop, and I love teaching, so here I am with 20 to 25 other people who like to talk about teaching and learning. ... You can take what you're learning and apply it immediately on the job and share it with your team members at school. You can get an idea on Monday and try it out in your classroom on Tuesday."

---

1. What grade level do you teach, how long have you been teaching, and what is the name of your school?
I've been teaching for 17 years. I teach third grade at Lakeville Elementary in Apopka, Florida.

2. Has the BrainSMART content been useful to you in your work as a classroom teacher?
Yes, very useful. I'm more able to read my students and help them learn the cognitive assets so they can be better learners. It empowers my students and helps them become self-motivated thinkers more willing to take chances because they realize they can learn using different methods and styles. It helped me earn my National Board Certification because the whole process made me a better thinker. The first time I went for it, I didn't make it. Then after I got my master's degree, I went for it a second time, and this time I was able to ace all my tests and finish the parts I did much better because I was able to apply a lot of the brain-based strategies through BrainSMART.

After earning my degree, I was named the Math Teacher of the Year at my school last year, Teacher of the Year at my school, and one of five finalists in Orange County along with three high school teachers and one other elementary school teacher. Orange County is one of the ten largest school systems in the United States, so that was quite an honor for me.

Applying all the BrainSMART strategies also helped me win a Best Buy Teacher Award three years in a row. You just write in about how you teach your kids using technology, and I focused on all the brain-based strategies I used. I got more than $7.000 that I get to spend on technology for my kids. I've also been awarded a Darden Grant for the last couple years I've been using a lot of the brain-based teaching strategies. I use technology to help the auditory and visual learners through videos.

I also applied for and received CitiGroup mentoring grant twice in a row. You mentor another teacher and help them learn how to read their students or work with auditory and visual learners, for example. We got tape recorders so the kids could hear themselves reading or read to other students and digital cameras to take pictures and document science experiments. The kids use those tools to apply to their learning, and they end up remembering more of what they learn.

3. What did you like about earning your degree 100% online?
It's perfect for a busy schedule because you can attend the class from anywhere in the world. You don't have to worry about going on vacations. I've been on vacation and been able to go to class. Or I've been at a PTA meeting where I could stay focused on that and still check in with class on the computer.

Another nice thing is that when you're taking the class at home, you don't have to worry about driving home after class. Once you're finished for the evening, you can just continue with your life.

And you get to meet people from all over the country, even all over the world. You learn about what's going on in classrooms in California, North Carolina, and Georgia. You find out there are a lot of issues that we're all having problems with, and we share ideas about what we're doing. It's kind of like a chat room, but even more useful. I like to talk shop, and I love teaching, so here I am with 20 to 25 other people who like to talk about teaching and learning. Some people may worry about not having face-to-face contact with peers, but you can take what you're learning and apply it immediately on the job and share it with your team members at school. You can get an idea on Monday and try it out in your classroom on Tuesday. It's very immediate.

4. How does this degree compare with other higher education programs you have studied?
For me, it's more practical. Right now, I'm getting a master's degree in reading, so I'm doing the reading and going to classes for the face-to-face. And I'm sharing the information. So it's similar, but BrainSMART is more practical for me because I can apply it to all the subjects I teach, not just the one I'm studying.

5. Would you recommend this program to other teachers?
Most definitely. As soon as I started about two or three summers ago, I recommended it to my friend, Sherry Genovese. She was going to a BrainSMART workshop led by Marcus, and I had signed up for another workshop on science. I accidentally went into the BrainSMART workshop and ended up crashing it when Marcus said I could attend. Then I found my friend Sherry there, and I told her all about my experience with the program, and the next thing you know, she started in the fall.

Last year I went to the Eric Jensen workshop, and I met a bunch of people there. I talked to a lady named Joanne Smith. She's yoga instructor, and I was telling her about the BrainSMART program. She said she was very interested, so I referred her to the Web site. I also met a guy named John from Taiwan, and I told him about it and sent his information to Mary. There are a couple teachers at my school who are interested, though they're not financially ready to go at this moment, but I've sent them all the information. I tell everybody about it.

6. What would you say about this program to other teachers?

First off, I tell them it's a fast way to get your master's degree. It only takes about 18 months. A lot of people say they're worried about writing, and I tell them not to worry about it because they're good writers. They're worried about the unknown. What is expected? I go through about five assignments. There's a discussion, and you do an artifact. It's all what you're learning about in the courses.

My favorite one was the second course about thinking and the cognitive assets. It's like you're teaching the kids to be empowered. You give them metacognitive processes and teach them how to be self-motivated thinkers. This course helps teachers make their students higher-level thinkers. It empowers them to learn. In my class, we go through all the 25 cognitive assets, and I train each of my kids on those assets. Before you know it, they're sitting there saying, "I was self-regulating. I knew you were talking, and I said to myself, 'Wait until she's finished speaking to interrupt her.'" The class I have now is just eating this stuff up. They're a sheltered English class, which means they think and speak in two languages. They just love to learn about the brain.

> "My favorite was the second course about thinking and the cognitive assets. It's like you're teaching the kids to be empowered. You give them metacognitive processes and teach them how to be self-motivated thinkers."
> —Tammy Daugherty

Some people say to me, "You never get any of the behavior problems." That's not true. If they could look at the kids before they come into my classroom, they would see that I end up with just as many challenges as anybody else. The difference is I teach the kids how to think for themselves. I let them know that they can learn, they just do so differently. We talk about the fact that some teachers teach to the auditory learners more than to the kinesthetic and visual learners, and then we talk about how you can cope with that and help yourself. I tell the kids you can't change the teachers, but you can help yourself because you're not always going to get the teachers who can accommodate your style of learning.

I just wish that when I was in high school, someone had taught me that. When I was in high school, I got my first radio and I started studying with my radio on, not knowing that I was an auditory learner. I thought I did better in high school because I was more motivated. I didn't realize until I was in the master's program that I could memorize faster when I added an auditory piece to my learning. My grades improved, but I didn't realize why until much later.

7. What would you say to an administrator about the program?
I talk to Dr. Kim Stutsman my principal about it all the time. She suggested that I spread the word, so we came up with a plan to do "Breakfast with the Brain." That is pretty easy because it's 7:30 to 8:00, only 30 minutes. People can make it there and then go about their business. We bring in the food, because that helps them come in, and then we come up with a topic of the day and I discuss it. Then they eat and discuss what they think about it.

My principal knows it's very important. We all went to the Brain Expos down here in Orlando. BrainSMART came to us about two years ago. I don't know if they're coming next year, but my principal is very interested in it. She knows she can put any student in my classroom and that child will be successful. The principal at the school where I taught before said the same thing. She said, "We need to get more teachers like Tammy because I can give her any student and they would be successful."

There's one little boy who I've known since kindergarten. The three teachers who've had him say he's been quite a challenge because he's very creative and a kinesthetic learner. They just don't know how to channel that energy, and so they react negatively toward him. I know he's an artist. I've already built a relationship. We've had tons of discussions. And I know that next year I want that young man in my classroom. I always want the challenging kids. It's not necessarily about control, just understanding them. If you read the third book in the BrainSMART series on the courageous learner, those are the children I like to teach. It has a chapter about reading the bar codes, understanding that some kids like to live in time and others like to live through time, that some like choices and some like to be told what to do. I know Mark likes choices. Other teachers say, "Mark can't do these. He won't do the work." I tell them to give him choices. For a writing assignment, he can write about this, this, or this. And I'll bet he'll do it because he'll have a choice. That gives him the impression that he has a little bit of control.

8. What would you say to a parent about the program?
I think parents like the program. As I'm working through the PTA and the School Advisory Council, they want me to do a session for parents, just a short thing. But I'm always sharing information about brain-based learning. Parents need to know their child can learn. They need to know that children learn in different ways. I was talking to a parent whose child was struggling in math, and we were talking about children with severe brain problems. Her daughter had told me there was a student at her other school who was retarded, and she wanted to know what that meant. I explained that with severe brain malfunctions, the brain might only mature to a certain age. Maybe the brain stops maturing at about five years old, so the child will never be able to do math or reading at a certain level. And then my student said, "Well, I'm not good at math, so does that mean that my brain is malfunctioning?" I told her, "You'll be able to do math. Your brain just needs to be wired to understand the concept. Right now you're not understanding the concept, but as you practice and practice, you're going to get smarter."

> "That's an important message for students and their parents. Sometimes kids don't make the connections right way, especially with reading. But once the coding part of their brain has been wired, they crack the code."
> —Tammy Daugherty

That's an important message for students and their parents. Sometimes kids don't make the connections right way, especially with reading. But once the coding part of their brain has been wired, they crack the code. I love that. You tell children that reading is a code, a mystery, and once you crack the code, you can move on. For instance, R is always going to be the R sound. Everywhere you see an R, that's what it will be. They come to understand that it's a code in a pattern, and their brain is a pattern seeker. So if they understand the patterns in reading and they're making their brain happy, they're going to get better at it.

Parents need to know that children need time to understand concepts and that they learn differently. If your kid is an auditory learner, buy them CDs with multiplication facts on them. Or if your kid is a visual learner and learning to read chapter books, that's a big thing. A parent might say, "My kid read a chapter book and didn't remember what happened." My advice would be to get some sticky notes and after each chapter, have them draw a picture or write a little summary and put that in there. Then before they move on to the next chapter, they can review their notes and look at the pictures to remember what happened in that chapter. By the time they get finished with the book, they'll know what's going on.

One other thing I like to tell parents is that it's OK for kids to use their fingers when they're reading when they're still in the concrete learner stage. Some people say don't do that, but I say let them use their fingers. It's their tool, their strategy to get through it. Once they finish with the concrete stage and move on to the abstract, that will go away. It's kind of like when you're learning to a tie your shoes, and your parents tell you the story about the bunny to help you remember what do to with the laces. Once they learn to tie their shoes, they don't need the bunny story anymore. Parents feel a lot better when they understand that their kids can learn.

9. What have you enjoyed most about the content?
I think I've enjoyed being able to reach each student. When we go over the barcodes, even with adults, you look at it and say, "Can you understand people more?" If you know somebody who lives through time and you're in time, you'll be able to understand that the other person might tend to be late and that all you need is a bit of patience. For the first four weeks of school, I don't nitpick or try to make the kids conform to certain things. I don't get on their case about it as they are getting used to the schedule. And if I have kids

that need to move around, I'll put them in the back of the room so they can get up if they need to without disrupting the other students. I get to know each student and teach them their learning style. Actually we discover it together. I don't tell them. I know it because I'm observing them, but letting the kids discover it and then helping them become independent thinkers helps them and me.

I no longer think of myself as the person who's teaching at the kids. I'm the facilitator and the kids are becoming independent learners using their skills. Hopefully, they teach me something. It just makes my classroom run smoother. We're a family, and it's not like I'm telling them everything to do.

10. Do you have a friend or colleague who took the program? What did they say about it?
My friend Sherry Genovese, who teaches at Audubon Elementary, said it was the best information she learned in 22 years of teaching. She said it's amazing that this is out there to help kids and she feels now that she can actually meet the needs of her children. Her favorite part of the BrainSMART program was the optimistic part. She loves the power of optimism, and she says that she has seen a lot of teachers who focus on the negative. She's trying to teach the kids and the teachers there that you need to have an optimistic outlook when it comes to learning. She would like to see more teachers use the BrainSMART strategy because it's really good stuff.

Denise Friedman
Earned: NSU M.S. focused on BrainSMART Teaching
"A day does not go by where I have not used something that I've been taught or something that I've learned through the BrainSMART program. I have a different attitude about my teaching now or a stronger feeling about what I've always believed education should be a about because of the program and the learning I've undertaken this year."

---

1. What grade level do you teach, how long have you been teaching, and what is the name of your school?
I am working toward a master's in education with a focus on brain research in NSU's BrainSMART program. I have taught for 13 years, the last ten as a thirdgrade teacher in Skokie, Illinois. Very rarely I teach fifth grade, depending on the year, and I privately tutor children in grades one through seven.

2. Has the content been useful to you in your work as a classroom teacher?
Content has been useful on a daily basis for me. A day does not go by where I have not used something that I've been taught or something that I've learned through the BrainSMART program. I have a different attitude about my teaching now or a stronger feeling about what I've always believed education should be a about because of the program and the learning I've undertaken this year. Many of the strategies and many of the bigger ideas that I've learned about this year I use when I am crafting an instructional unit, speaking with a student, speaking with a colleague, or thinking about anything that has to do with my teaching or also when I think of myself as a teacher.

The most recent example of a child's aha moment is providing the right amount of visual support for a student I have who is a strong visual learner but also has severe auditory processing difficulties. That has made all the difference in bringing down their anxiety about learning in general and I found the key and was able to open that child up, who had a lot more inside when I started using a lot more visual support. I will draw out a vocabulary in a graphic organizer, they will give their input into it before they have to listen to or read a story. When they were listening, there were so many things they were not hearing or weren't able to follow the story. If you can't follow the story you can't take part in a discussion afterward. It has made our relationship much better, too. It was the piece they needed in order to feel I was totally on their side, wanting their success. I knew they weren't quite getting everything they needed from the lesson and once the visual piece fell into place, their learning was so much better.

3. What do you like about earning your degree 100% online?
The things I love most about online learning is how truly convenient it is to not have to attend a master's program at night, find parking and have to leave my house during the most important time for my family. I don't have to be away from them. After teaching a full day to then have to go to a physical classroom instead of a virtual classroom would have been impossible for me to do and I am grateful this is offered online. I find it thorough and the way it was presented originally caught me. This fit my expectations for a master's program and I have not been disappointed.

4. How does this degree compare with other higher education programs you have studied?
I think this program has moved past the bulletin board-decorations and sing-songs, all the stuff that many teachers like to take away. It has also moved past all the theory with no application part of many of the higher education courses. BrainSMART has found an almost perfect balance between what we need to know and what we need to do to be effective teachers regardless of one's personal style. That's all about the bulletin board and it didn't make it seem like another ditto to hand out, that "give it to me" kind of stuff. This makes everyone step up, if you want something, you have to craft it yourself. Keep it off the flat curriculum. It totally steered clear of that.

5. Would you recommend this program to other teachers?
Yes, and I have.

6. What would you say to other teachers about the program?
It is profoundly priceless. Even though it is very economical to do this program, it certainly tests and stretches your definition of what teaching is. It has clearly and very specifically helped me point out the things in myself that needed to change and for that I will always be grateful.

I could have gone on knowing things weren't working but not pushing myself to change it and this program helped me do that. Like a workout coach, do it again, and you really don't want to do it at all. It's much easier to sit and complain and this really changed my family, my students and me. I think knowing more about how everyone's brains work, was such a concrete thing, that first set of classes that were about brain function and nutrition, you start out with brain architecture, this is what we know about our bodies.

I have a fifth grade boy and a third grade girl, I'm 43, and I see them as more whole. As the classes progressed, from very concrete, to now we are talking about abstract concepts like respect. We try to make it somewhat concrete, like this is what I say and do, it moved me from seeing my children as processing machines to seeing how incredibly unique they are and the beauty of that, and to moving toward true communication with them, with much more conscious respect. I would think and choose my words much more carefully with my own children because I really do see how a small utterance can make a difference in children's lives. I wanted it to be my children too because they didn't get what they needed in the private schools I chose, and my children have suffered from the global dysfunction of the education system. This has affected my children in a great way, more organic, I'm much healthier now, I do yoga now, I lost over 20 pounds, and my husband also did and it is just different now. Our lives are different now. I searched for this and I'm ready for this and I'm very picky about what I choose.

7. What would you say to an administrator about the program?
She sees how great it is, she offers me very special things because she sees how passionate I am about teaching, I'll be attending a workshop in Cleveland that she found funding for, pairs up with differentiated instruction, I am the classroom and the teacher she chose, to be part of a professional development video this year.

8. What would you say to parents?
My parents were very supportive and pushed for me to loop with their kids, so I am. I'll be looping with my class. The parents have really

heard me when I spoke to them about nutrition, I brought in a nutritionist and the parents have become very committed to this. I have a lot of communication with my parents, I speak with them on the phone, also when they pick up their children from school. This kind of learning breaks the tradition that "I hate school" that many of them suffered from. They are grateful and have communicated to me that they hated school and are thrilled that their children loved school this year. That's all they wanted. I make lists of recommended books, web sites, I research certain topics for them and I think they are very happy that I chose to do BrainSMART. Some are educators and they are also very supportive.

9. What have you enjoyed the most about the content?
My favorite text was *The Language of Respect*. It made me cry and I spoke to the author and expressed how moving I found it to be. I had to read it twice, and took fifty pages of notes on it. It spoke to me. That book really spoke to me. I loved that text more than anything. Another part of the content that I enjoyed, I loved the accelerated learning. Loved, loved crafting my lesson plans based on that book. Changed my life and lesson plans. It runs through the entire program, about the body-brain connection, the nutrition, the idea of brains being different but each one needs to be respected and supported, loved that idea. In every way that Marcus has provided information about it, and also Donna's presentation. I love the videos.

10. Did you have a friend or colleague who took the program? What did they say about the program?
I did not. I hope the word will spread.

Marlene Mendes
Earned: NSU M.S. in BrainSMART Teaching
"I had a student who had a very negative attitude. I talked to her about it and asked her to name three positive things, trying to get her to focus on being positive. She's turned around."

---

1. What grade level do you teach, how long have you been teaching, and what is the name of your school?
I teach physical education with secondary students in San Luis Obispo, California. I have been teaching for 31 years and previously taught elementary and middle school students. I am pursuing a Master's degree at Nova Southeastern University with a concentration in brain-based education.

2. Has the content been useful to you in your work as a classroom teacher?
On two occasions, a concept helped in the class. Both instances dealt with optimism—a student's and mine. I had a student who had a very negative attitude. I talked to her about it and asked her to name three positive things, trying to get her to focus on being positive. She's turned around. She's dressing out and participating. She's involved and a lot less negative.

Another girl had a lot of trouble following choreography in dance aerobics, so we stayed very positive, made a big deal of complimenting her when she took a risk and did something new. I've tried to give her some choices and also tried to stay optimistic about it. Today she actually did the beginning of our program— the warm-up. One of the girls has taken an interest in her and has been supportive, and that has helped, too.

The series and ideas have been great. Since I teach high school physical education, it is always a challenge to find presentation strategies that teenagers will accept. They are such a tough audience.

3. What do you like about earning your degree 100% online?
I really enjoy the convenience of online and that convenience is why I can now get my master's degree.

4. How does this degree compare with other higher education programs you have studied?
I like that the program has so much substance and it progresses so quickly. It is not dragged out.

5. Would you recommend this program to other teachers?
Yes. The concepts are very important and they make sense. The
brain can ready the learner to be a better student. It can decrease
depression and I have even incorporated the program into my
dance aerobics. The state
of the learner is very
important and has been
ignored for far too long by
most districts. This
program provides great
data and evidence about the academic relevance of physical
education for our young people.

> "Personally, I would love to see my entire school get the information about the state of the learner, as well as the district leadership and the school board."
> —Marlene Mendes

6. What would you say to other teachers about the program?
That it would depend on their grade level but there are great
concepts, ideas, and lessons depending on the grade level you
teach and your creativity. The variations in modality of learning
hit more than just reading and the kinesthetic learner, so that's
great. The research is fairly new and a lot of us who went through
didn't have access to the brain and cognitive research we can use
today.

7. What would you say to an administrator about the program?
Personally, I would love to see my entire school get the
information about the state of the learner, as well as the district
leadership and the school board. I'd like everyone to have a good
idea of the benefit of physical education when they make long-
range plans so they can see the carry-over benefit to the
classroom—students with better attention spans, improved
memory, and it goes on and on. Our school has fairly high test
scores already.

8. What would you say to parents?
I would stress the state of the learner as well as the various
strategies, that the strategies are beneficial to their children.

Dewey Hooper

Earned: NSU M.S. in BrainSMART Teaching

"Without hesitation I would recommend that other teachers get into this brain-based cognitive program. It is an exceptionally well-organized program that will help recharge the passion for helping kids learn."

1. What grade level do you teach, how long have you been teaching, and what is the name of your school?

I have been teaching for ten years, and currently teach physical education at Savannah Christian Preparatory School in Savannah, Georgia. I completed a Master's degree in the Fall of 2006 concentrating in BrainSMART.

2. Has the content been useful to you in your work as a classroom teacher?

It has changed the way I formulate and present my lessons. I allow more time for the kids to think and observe before asking them to respond. It's fun to watch their eyes move up as they activate the part of the brain associated with memory, as they in that moment recall information I taught them.

3. What do you like about earning your degree 100% online?

It's been a blessing to be able to learn in my own home instead of driving back and forth after a day of work to the closest program. The convenience is great, saves time and energy, very easy and accommodating.

4. How does this degree compare with other higher education programs you have studied?

These brain-based programs at Nova Southeastern University are challenging and convenient, but not impossibly difficult. I enjoyed the scientific parts, learning about brain-based and cognitive research and educational techniques. Learning an entirely new orientation toward education was stimulating.

5. Would you recommend this program to other teachers?

Without hesitation I would recommend that other teachers get into this brain-based cognitive program. It is an exceptionally well-organized program that will help recharge the passion for helping kids learn.

6. What would you say to other teachers about the program?
If you're looking for something challenging and exciting, get in. You will learn a tremendous amount about how people learn. Our pastor once said he took 25 years of sermons and threw them out to start over with a fresh outlook. That's what I have done with my lesson plans—thrown them out and started fresh with the new techniques I have learned in the program.

7. What would you say to an administrator about the program?
BrainSMART programs help educators gain confidence and leadership skills, and that translates into more satisfied teachers and more productive classroom learning. It will improve your teachers' morale, which will energize the environment and set off a reaction that will end in better outcomes for the kids.

8. What would you say to parents?
I would want my child's teacher to be a BrainSMART teacher. I know a BrainSMART-trained educator will help my child taking their individual needs into account, because they have the knowledge and skills to deliver individual instruction to larger classrooms without sacrificing quality.

9. What have you enjoyed the most about the content?
I have enjoyed specific aspects of learning styles. For example, it's obvious that my work as a physical education teacher involves kinesthetic learning, but so much visual and auditory content is involved too. I know how the body and health powerfully influences learning and the brain, but it was powerful to be able to match up data about how various lifestyle choices, like nutrition and activity level, can help our children thrive intellectually. I know what I do is important but this helps me quantify that with data for my peers and for my own sense of accomplishment.

10. Did you have a friend or colleague who took the program? What did they say about the program?
Between my wife and myself, we have several family members who have joined the program, as well as coworkers. We all enjoy the sense of competence and control brain-based teaching gives us.

Edna Gibson
Earned: NSU M.S. BrainSMART Teaching
"BrainSMART is how I thought learning to be a teacher should be. I really thought I would have learned these things when I was in my fifth year of studying to be a teacher."

1. What grade level do you teach, how long have you been teaching, and what is the name of your school?
I teach eighth-grade physical science. I've been a teacher for 20 years. I work at Richard L. Graves Middle School in Whittier, California.

2. Has the BrainSMART content been useful to you in your work as a classroom teacher?
Yes it has. When I attended college, I was credentialed as a home economics teacher, but the only time I ever taught home economics when I did my student teaching. I was offered a job where I am now, and I taught computers, mainly keyboarding, for 10 years. I didn't know programming, but I taught students how to keyboard and I could type 90 words a minute, so I was pretty successful at that. The students were always engaged, and they never had any behavior problems. They loved my class, they loved computers and the programs, and they loved me. Then with No Child Left Behind, they got rid of computer class. In 2003 they told me I could teach eighth-grade physical science because I have a bachelor of science in home economics and I took a physics class and chemistry class one time. So now that's what I'm teaching.

You would not believe how horrible it was for me until I took the BrainSMART program. I would go to the principal and say, "I don't know how to teach this. What do I do?" I didn't understand what they meant by teaching to the standards. I didn't even understand how to use the textbook. The book was just like college level for eighth graders. It was stuff I studied in college. None of the other staff would help me because it's a really competitive situation, and everyone wants to be the number one teacher.

All I knew how to do was have them read the chapter. I knew about directed reading and thinking activities because I took a reading class in college. That's mostly what I did: teach them how to read the book. But I didn't know how to give them hands-on activities or anything. It was truly a living nightmare. I had the National Teachers Association Magazine come to my house four times a year, and I saw a little ad on BrainSMART. The BrainSMART ad said, "Read your students' barcode for their brain. See how they think. See how they learn best." Those were the types of things I had been asking for years and begging people to help me with. I was trying to teach myself how to do it, but I couldn't do it on my own. The BrainSMART program went beyond my expectations. I didn't expect to learn as much as I have. I didn't expect it to be easy for me to understand, but it made sense to me from the very start.

It always made sense to me because I was always trying to do curriculum development. People would tell me, "You have to do hands-on activities." I would see kids in other classes who were doing things, but they didn't seem to be learning anything. I could see that it was never making a connection in their minds. When I would ask what they were doing in those other classes, they didn't know. They just said they were having fun. But with the strategies I have now, we talk about what we're doing and what we're going to learn and

> "It always made sense to me because I was always trying to do curriculum development. … With the strategies I have now, we talk about what we're doing and what we're going to learn and how it all connects with previous experiences."
> —Edna Gibson

how it all connects with previous experiences.

3. What did you like about earning your degree 100% online?
I'm partially handicapped so it's hard for me to get around. I had an accident 10 years ago so I don't drive on the freeway. I live in California and I just told myself when I got injured that I was never going to get a master's degree. Physically, I just did not have what it took to get myself to and from a university. My husband would have been willing to drive me, but then he would have had to stay there for two or three hours and then drive me back home. The college nearest our home is only 12 miles away, but it can take an hour to two hours to get there because of the LA traffic.

The superintendent of our school suggested that I take an online course. But I had heard other people talking about online programs, and they sounded like "diploma mills," I guess they call them. I didn't want a degree bad enough that I would go to a diploma mill. I wanted to learn something.

BrainSMART is how I thought learning to be a teacher should be. I really thought I would have learned these things when I was in my fifth year of studying to be a teacher. I was surprised and disappointed that none of the universities I had attended taught me how to teach. But with BrainSMART I had classes that actually taught me how to be a teacher.

4. How does this degree compare with other higher education programs you've studied?
It's in a league of its own. All universities should have to teach that way—or at least give teachers the option. Would you like to learn how to teach and how kids think? Or do you just want to go through this mindless programming? I don't mean to sound so bitter about it, but after what I've learned and what I was never taught before, it just makes me mad, with all the wasted years and all the fear and anxiety I had. Now I don't have any of those problems anymore. Some of my colleagues have even told the vice principal that now I seem happy. I didn't even realize that I seemed unhappy before, but I was worried sick for five years. Worried sick

about losing my job. Worried sick about those test scores. My students' scores went up 8% on the state test, and that before I even got to the Thinking for Results and differentiated instruction part of the program. I'm learning this as I go, and I'm doing a bit at a time, but already their test cores are up 8%.

I completed the program in December, so in January, I'm just going to start doing the Thinking for Results on a daily basis, teaching those cognitive assets. Even if my students are not really interested in physics or chemistry, they're fascinated when I tell them things about their brain. For instance, students are supposed to memorize the first 30 elements on the Periodic Table. It's a standards thing. One thing I was able to with the kids was use that power of color where they focus on the color of the different regions so that they know what the metals are and the nonmetals.

Here's another strategy that works. When I would give an oral exam on the Periodic Table, some of the kids get stuck around element 14 or 16. So I told them what Marcus Conyers says to do: Look up to your right, which accesses your occipital lobe. It was the most amazing thing I ever saw, like magic or something. I would tell the kids, "Remember this when you get stuck: Look up to your right." They're kind of shy, and some of them didn't want to do it. I said, "Just try it." So they would, and within a second or two, they would remember and go on and complete the whole thing. It sounds corny, doesn't it? But it works. And they like it. I had a student last year when I first heard about looking up and I told him to do it. A couple months later, after I'd forgotten about sharing that with him, he said, "Mrs. Gibson, every time I get stuck, I look up and I get the answer."

> "Some of my kids from last year who are in high school now came back to tell me that they got really high scores on their science test with the state of California. ... [They] said they'd never gotten such a high score in their lives. I told them, 'Just remember these strategies and you'll do well your whole life.'"
> —Edna Gibson

Some of my kids from last year who are in high school now came back to tell me that they got really high scores on their science test with the state of California. That really surprised me because some of these kids were just C and B students, not the A students. The A students did well, too, but I expected that they would. These other kids said they'd never gotten such a high score in their lives. I told them, "Just remember these strategies and you'll do well your whole life." It was really fascinating to hear and so great that they'd make the effort to come back and tell me.

5. Would you recommend this program to other teachers?
Sure, I think everyone should have to take it.

6. What would you say about the program to other teachers?
First, it teaches them how someone learns best and which style that a child will learn best. This has an impact on discipline, too. Discipline is disorganized at the school where I teach. We don't have a vice principal in charge of that, so teachers all handle it differently. If kids act out, they get sent to this one classroom and they sit there all day. If all the teachers understand that students need to be taught in a way they can learn, I don't think we'd have as many discipline problems. I'm certain that when they realize they can learn, they would start acting better.

7. What would you say to an administrator about the program?
I think administrators should learn about the BrainSMART strategies and have workshops and encourage all teachers to learn this. About three years ago, a group of teachers went through another program and gave us all two little supplemental packets on its teaching strategies. On an in-service day, these people came and showed us a PowerPoint presentation and discussed the different strategies. But what happens where I work—and it probably happens in other places, too—is that they'll have a workshop on a good program, but they never pursue it or teach us how to apply it. I just completed a class on classroom management and increasing student achievement, and two of the books were from the same program, but it went into much greater detail and the BrainSMART teachers really taught us how to use graphic organizers. They did a much better job of presenting that

information than in the original workshop. If I didn't have the textbooks from that workshop, I would not have believed it was the same author. It was a night-and-day difference in the knowledge the professors shared and the techniques they use to teach.

Here's another example. I was having a problem with some kids implementing Thinking for Results. They didn't truly understand it. I would administer the assessment, and the kids would answer the questions, but the results were the opposite of what I actually see going in on my class. They were nice kids, but they just could not do the work. I thought something must be wrong here, so I wrote my professor, Dr. Joye Norris, and she recommended a book by Betty K. Garner called *Getting to Got It: Helping Struggling Students Learn How to Learn.* I think this should be a required text, because it was so helpful. The author used one example of a student looking at a drawing of an octagon, but he saw a box. It shows how the kid added extra lines in his mind to get a box. So I went to school and in each of my classes, I drew that shape on the board and asked the students to raise their hand and say what they saw. I asked if anyone saw anything different and sure enough at least five to seven kids per class saw a box instead of an octagon. I asked each of those kids to come up and draw what they saw on the board. It was amazing.

I teach a lot of kids—215 a day. That's another reason I'm so excited. You have so many kids, and so many are failing because no one knows how to teach to their learning style. Using BrainSMART, I've been able to coach those kids and help them so that they could at least get up to a C in the class and do some work.

8. What would you say to a parent about the program?
I remember talking to the father of one boy who would do nothing in class. He's a bright kid, but he wasn't going to do anything if he could get away with it. I told his father about BrainSMART and how we're teaching students to drive their own brains, and that's exactly what the father said, "That's what I want. I want him to drive his own brain." That father just loved that I was teaching the kids to think for themselves and drive their own brains. He'd call

me once a month and say, "Has John been driving his own brain yet?"

I had another student who was a behavioral problem. His dad came in, and he was upset about his son's progress report. His son had told him I was the meanest teacher in the whole school, the whole nine yards. I told the father that the boy was talking all the time, but I taught him what we call the H.E.A.R. strategy, and I told him about my university and how we learn to use these strategies. I asked the student to tell his father about the hearer strategy, and he was able to repeat verbatim how to use it to his father. Right then and there, his dad saw that it wasn't the class or the teacher that was the problem. After that, the kid started doing his work. I guess his father went home and talked to him about using those strategies in school. The parents are interested in how and what their kids are learning. They really are. We tell them it's a community: the students, the teachers, the parents, and the administration all working together to help kids learn.

9. What have you enjoyed most about the BrainSMART content?
I enjoyed learning the cognitive assets. They each have a name, so I'm able to think about them, I'm able to implement them, and I'm able to see results. Before I started with BrainSMART, those kids were getting a 32% classroom average on those benchmark tests. You probably could have been blindfolded and scored higher. Since I started learning this last year, my classes went up to 50%, and some of them went up to more than 70%—and that was before I completed all the classes. Starting in January, now that I'm done with the coursework, I really expect those scores to go up to at least 70 to 80% in each class—in all six of them, not just one or two.

One strategy I love is called a pictogram. It's featured in *The Accelerated Learning Handbook* by Dave Meier, one of the books we studied in our differentiated learning class. It follows the rule that BrainSMART teaches you that 20% of what you do gives you 80% of the results. I share that with my students. I say, "How would you like to work less and score better?" We have the kids go through a standards review workbook about a month before the state test. Before I introduce each new unit, I have them make these pictograms. For example, Standard 3 is on solids, liquids, or gas, so they have to know the physical properties and appearances and chemical properties of each state of matter. How do they know if it's a chemical reaction or a physical change? When water freezes or turns into steam, how do they know if that's chemical or physical? By creating a pictogram, it helps them get an idea in their mind about how when water is boiling, it might change its appearance and form but it did not happen chemically. It happens physically like if you smash a marshmallow with your hand, it's still a marshmallow, but if you toast it and it burns, that's a chemical reaction. I have them draw pictures of each standard and the strand for each unit. They keep them with them, and I post the best ones on the wall as a basis to discuss what we're learning in class. The kids love them. They always want to know when they're doing pictograms again.

10. Did you have a friend or colleague who took the program?
No I didn't know anyone who took it. But I'll tell you, I had done a PowerPoint on Marzano's nine keys for raising student achievement for my 699 research class, and my department chair for science loves that presentation. He wants to go over to the school district and show all the different strategies and techniques to the school board. The vice principal wants me to give a workshop for our staff. Now it's just a matter of getting everyone to being able to teach that way.

Lisa M. Tanner
Earned: NSU M.S. BrainSMART Teaching
"There was so much useful content that seemed to fit with who I am as a teacher. It just works for me....I researched a lot of programs, and they all sounded so monotonous and boring to me. These studies focused on the research, whole-body learning and the whole child."

1. What grade level do you teach, how long have you been teaching, and what is the name of your school?
I'm in my seventh year of teaching, currently as the K-5 math specialist at Brayton Elementary School with North Adams Public Schools in North Adams, Massachusetts. I completed the BrainSMART program in 2003.

2. Has the BrainSMART content been useful to you in your work as a classroom teacher?
I really have found that it is really useful. The way the content works is that it embodies whole child teaching—the physical and emotional aspects, as well as the academic. I try to use as much of that program as I can.

3. What did you like about earning your degree 100% online?
I was a single mom at the time and working full time. It afforded me the opportunity to do the work when I had the time. I didn't have to run home, cook dinner and then leave my son with someone else. Granted, for 16 months, I had no life. I probably wrote more papers in that 16 months than most people write in their entire lives. I had to be committed. I had deadlines to meet. I had to be online talking to my professor and classmates. There were deadlines and requirements, but I could fit my life around them.

Another plus was that I live in the middle of nowhere, so driving to a university to take courses would have taken a lot more time. The opportunity to earn my degree online just really worked for me.

4. How does this degree compare with other higher education programs you have studied?
It was intensive. There was so much useful content that seemed to fit with who I am as a teacher. It just works for me. In the state of Massachusetts, teachers have five years to start a master's program after they get their teaching certification. I researched a lot of programs, and they all sounded so monotonous and boring to me. These studies focused on the research, whole-body learning and the whole child. It was fairly new and innovative.

5. Would you recommend this program to other teachers?
I'm always talking about how much I loved that program. I recommend it to other teachers. Most of the people I'm with now already have their degrees. Others are choosing to specialize in special education or reading, because the Department of Education in Massachusetts is telling them they have to specialize. Back when I was in the program, they wanted you to get a master's degree. But within the past year, especially for teachers who waited to start working on a master's degree, they're steering them toward very specific programs.

6. What would you say to other teachers about the program?
I still tell people about the program all the time—and how much I got out of it. It really struck a chord with me, and I decided, "This is the way I want to teach." It really is a magnificent program, and I use what I learned all the time.

7. What would you say to an administrator about the program?
Last year, we had a professional development program, and they brought in a speaker and consultant. After the program, I told people, "That's exactly what my master's program was about."

8. What would you say to parents?

We're dealing with a lot of parent apathy. We struggle with trying to get parents involved. We always try to come up with innovative ways to bring them to the school, but it gets harder and harder.

9. What have you enjoyed the most about the content?

I like that it's doable. It's applicable. It's not so far out there. A lot of strategies just make sense. They're logical, common sense, and they're all based on research.

> "On occasion, if I feel like I'm stuck on something, I take the BrainSMART manuals out and go through them."
> —Lisa M. Tanner

On occasion, if I feel like I'm stuck on something, I take the BrainSMART manuals out and go through them. I keep those books on my bookshelf in my class. I look through the strategies. They don't just collect dust. I use them for ways to connect with my class and to certain students.

10. Did you have a friend or colleague who took the program? What did they say about it?

When I started the NSU program, I ended up snagging one of my colleagues, and she took it with me. And after I finished, I talked to another colleague who ended up enrolling in the program. Every time she sees me, she still thanks me for recommending it. She says it was one of the best graduate programs she's even taken.

Motivating Middle School Minds with BrainSMART

Impassioned educator Christina Issac has never shied away from a challenge—like focusing her talents on tumultuous 'tweens in middle school. Issac has taught for six years, all with middle school students, and is currently teaching sixth graders at Washington Middle School in Cairo, Georgia.

Christina Issac
Earned: NSU M.S.
BrainSMART Teaching
With their hormones in full fluctuation, it is easy for middle school students to become moody and pessimistic. But aided by visuals of an ant carrying a watermelon, Issac keeps the kids focused on their brains' tremendous potential for learning and achievement.

Issac says BrainSMART retention strategies have transformed her classroom, including inclusion students in special education. Her students are allowed to look up during tests, to activate the visual part of the brain that is connected to memory.

Practical optimism and the EFFORT strategy help get her adolescent students in a receptive mindset for learning. With their hormones in full fluctuation, it is easy for this age group to become moody and pessimistic. But aided by visuals of an ant carrying a watermelon, Issac keeps the kids focused on their brains' tremendous potential for learning and achievement.

Issac earned a Master of Science degree with a specialization in BrainSMART Teaching and Learning from Nova Southeastern University. She encourages other educators to look into the BrainSMART program, saying it helps teachers earn the respect and pay increases they deserve, and it will help equip them to reach more children with diverse needs and learning styles. It's easy to get complacent in the classroom and this is a new way to look at teaching and a new way to reach children.

Earned: NSU M.S. BrainSMART Teaching

"I was excited and stunned to learn that cognitive skills can be learned. ...Teaching kids the cognitive skills has been instrumental in helping them feel successful in what they're doing and getting them motivated to learn."

1. What grade level do you teach, how long have you been teaching, and what is the name of your school?

I primarily teach fifth graders at Bartow County Public Schools' Allatoona Elementary School in Acworth, Georgia. I am certified K-12 in Special Education, K-8 in math, language arts, social studies, and science.

2. Has the content been useful to you in your work as a classroom teacher?

Absolutely. My instruction centers around attention, transfer, and retention of information. I create a safe, motivating environment in the classroom. Kids come in with varying degrees of readiness at the start of the day, and a lot of that has to do with the home in the morning. So I start with SMART to hook them into a learning frame of mind.

D'Jon McNair

I place a lot of emphasis on understanding the science behind Thinking for Results. How can I deliver lessons at input-output, how do kids think, and why is it important to have cognitive skills at various levels? I was excited and stunned to learn that cognitive skills can be learned. Clear intent states that "I know what I'm going to do next." That course was instrumental in teaching me that many of the things I took for granted that kids know, they don't, and if we're going to talk about clear intent, for instance, what should the next thing that I do. Teaching kids the cognitive skills has been instrumental in helping kids feel successful in what they're doing and getting them motivated to learn.

While I was working through the Courageous Learners material, I happened to get a troubled student in my class with a long history of behavioral issues. I strove to reach this child and decided to invest a lot of time establishing our relationship. Until they're comfortable with you, kids aren't interested in opening up like that. Everyday I read the child "The More You Do, The More You Can Do," because it was a lack of effort that caused a lot of problems for him in the

> "You should have seen the expression on the child's face when he was called to accept his award and realized he was being recognized. He is still doing very well."
> — D'Jon McNair

past. I tied his personal interests into our classroom material, for example, asking him to consider what it would have been like to fly a prop plane as an explorer in the 1800s during America's time of territorial expansion. I had to allow him some literary freedom to write about what it would be like to fly over a covered wagon. He could tie necessary facts to something more expressive that he wanted to add to it. Because he didn't read on grade level, he was significantly behind. I allowed him to do verbal lessons because he was an auditory learner. When I think of any of the kids I've worked with, he's the one who stands out, because he went from being reevaluated for a behavioral disability to learning what he needed to learn and even won an award from a local civic group in only nine weeks. You should have seen the expression on the child's face when he was called to accept his award and realized he was being recognized. He is still doing very well. He has accommodations for the statewide test we're getting ready to take and he's been scoring up to the 70th percentile, which is a passing score. We always try to keep a positive perspective; you got more than 50 percent. You have learned more. You have achieved more. Let's keep trying to improve.

The culmination and sequence of the BrainSMART courses has

been extremely important in how I approach things in the classroom. There are situations where we are required to follow state guidelines on timing of a subject in the curriculum. BrainSMART allows me to think outside the box. My co-teacher in math and I were able to design an activity to allow kids to go shopping, to allow kids real life experiences. What is a better deal—one of each or two for one, based on price? The kids were really motivated to do this with their parents the next year. We have them collect the ads from three different stores, and they worked together to find out where they'd save the most money. It connected to state standards and yet kept them engaged.

3. What do you like about earning your degree 100% online?
I like the flexibility, not having to travel and having access to the content and curriculum online. I am involved with our region's Special Olympics, heavily involved in the church and also coach baseball, so the online program allowed me to put in a couple hours as an independent learner and it was conducive to my learning style. My peers have been reluctant to embrace online because they require face-to-face contact, but I have been able to study with a mini-cohort from my own school so anyone considering an online degree can feel highly confident that having a few peers involved as a cohort would help you feel more connected.

4. How does this degree compare with other higher education programs you have studied?
The BrainSMART curriculum ties into what I do as a special education teacher, as far as the science and education of learning. I was taught the art of learning but not the science, and BrainSMART gives me the science of what's new about brain research. I considered a Master's degree in Special Education, but it would have been a repeat and I needed something different. The BrainSMART program has been a wise investment and choice when compared to my alternatives in a traditional degree program. Many of my peers who pursued on-campus traditional degrees say they have wasted their time and money because, although they will receive a pay raise for this attainment, they were not able to turn

that information around and use it in the classroom. Every bit of information I learned in the program has been immediately useful in my classrooms.

5. Would you recommend this program to other teachers?
I highly recommend BrainSMART programs to my colleagues. I look at new teachers just coming in and ones who are struggling and I've been able to share some of the information with peers. You can see the light go on in their head. They come back and say, "That really worked." It gives me an opportunity to talk more about my program of study.

6. What would you say to other teachers about the program?
This coursework will help you understand the science of learning and what you can do on a daily basis to impact your kids in a positive way. BrainSMART techniques will be instrumental in helping students improve their successes and academic achievements. If you want to improve your teaching skills, this is the program you need to consider. I have about six colleagues seriously considering enrolling in the program. We had 30–40 teachers for the info session, and more than half signed up for the program.

7. What would you say to an administrator about the program?
I've had a chance to share my portfolio with my principal and assistant principal, and I use the terminology "proof in the pudding." I've encouraged them to encourage other teachers to look at and consider the program.

8. What would you say to parents?
Wow. That's a good question. My philosophy is this: regardless of who the kid is, what their family circumstance, what issues they bring to the school, positive or negative, once they enter that door, they're ours. We have to do everything we can possibly do in the five or six hours we have them to help them achieve to their potential. I would tell a parent it's inherent in skills, my strategies, and me. I hear a lot of complaints from my peers about the kids not able to learn because of what's happening in the home. I don't

want to blame anyone else. Kids spend almost 90 percent of their lives with the family, we get them for about 13 percent of the time, and we have to optimize that time 100 percent of the time by not complaining about things we have no control over.

> "Our technology teacher in the BrainSMART program will be adding to the computers a front page where kids can come in and ... do a learning styles survey. ... [Teachers] will have individual student and classroom profiles based on learning styles, and it will also incorporate Thinking for Results into the survey."
> — D'Jon McNair

9. What have you enjoyed the most about the content?
One thing I enjoyed most about the coursework and the information were the additional resources Donna and Marcus provide in their study guides. The literature provided cites the research and links to external Web sites that further delved into concepts and studies woven into the BrainSMART program.

10. Did you have a friend or colleague who took the program? What did they say about the program?
Mark, our technology teacher in the BrainSMART program, will be adding to the computers a front page where kids can come in and, as they do initial rotations, they will do a learning styles survey. Mark will get that data back to the homeroom teachers who can disseminate that to teachers so they can better target kids. They will have individual student and classroom profiles based on learning styles, and it will also incorporate Thinking for Results into the survey.

This program been the best dollar investment I've made in my kids and myself.

Breean Thurber
Earned: NSU M.S. BrainSMART Teaching
"In my first year of teaching, I was positive and excited, and as the years have gone by, enthusiasm has waned. BSL (brain-based education) is helping me become a better teacher in general.... Also being able to interact with teachers from other parts of the country is interesting, how different regions and districts do things differently."

1. What grade level do you teach, how long have you been teaching, and what is the name of your school?
I teach fourth graders at Gilbert Magnet School, in the Clark County Public School District in Clark County, Nevada. I have been teaching for five years. I started earning my master's degree with a concentration in BrainSMART in June 2006 and will complete it in August 2007.

2. Has the content been useful to you in your work as a classroom teacher?
Since I work at a magnet school, I try to teach with multiple intelligences, and BSL has made me become a better teacher. In my first year of teaching, I was positive and excited, and as the years have gone by, enthusiasm has waned. BSL is helping me become a better teacher in general. How important what I say is to the kids and how personally they receive everything I say. I am careful with my words and try to be as positive as possible.

3. What do you like about earning your degree 100% online?
I like it because of the convenience. Also being able to interact with teachers from other parts of the country is interesting, how different regions and districts do things differently. I find this very beneficial for my own reflection. Not having to drive anywhere, I am a visual learner so this is better for me, anyway.

4. How does this degree compare with other higher education programs you have studied?
I am helping my boyfriend do an online program, and I hate the format of his program. Instructions are vague, there is no interaction between him and his professors. His program is

atrocious. I thought all online programs were as complete and effective as mine.

5. *Would you recommend this program to other teachers?*
I have recommended it to a few colleagues who are interested in an online advanced degree. Because of the focus of our magnet program, which is creative arts, it fits well with our teaching needs. Some who have topped out on their pay scales have considered this as a way to take their career and compensation farther.

6. *What would you say to other teachers about the program?*
The readings are beneficial, the chats are important, just because you get to bounce ideas off other teachers and get differing viewpoints from people you don't usually interact with from different parts of the country.

7. *What would you say to an administrator about the program?*
I actually talked to my administrator about this during my evaluation and told her I am getting a lot from the program.

8. *What would you say to parents?*
Each student has different strengths and by taking these courses I am able to hit more of their strengths and help them with the areas that need attention. This gives me specific, implementable ideas to help me work with them.

9. *What have you enjoyed the most about the content?*
I liked the first class about the physiology of the brain. The mapping the mind book is my favorite of all so far. After that, Dr. Joye was probably the most involved of the professors. She gave us a lot of feedback and was very specific and encouraging when we worked on different things. She gave a lot of support.

10. Did you have a friend or colleague who took the program? What did they say about the program?
I've shared the program with a few colleagues and my administrator.

Interviews with Teacher Leaders: Educational Specialist Degree

Heather C. Toner
Earned: NSU Ed.S. in BrainSMART Teaching

"Learning about the science of the brain and having tools to use to differentiate instruction based on the principles of how the brain functions is undeniably critical to teaching."

1. What grade level do you teach, how long have you been teaching, and what is the name of your school?
I teach 9-12 ESOL (English for Speakers of Other Languages) at Peachtree Ridge High School in Suwanee, Georgia. This is my 15th year of teaching; I have spent my time along the way as a bilingual elementary teacher, a middle and high school Spanish teacher, and the last five years as an ESOL teacher and department chair.

2. Has the content been useful to you in you work as a classroom teacher?
The BrainSMART content has revolutionized how I teach, and what I can bring to enhance student performance and language acquisition. It has enabled me to more effectively serve and support my students and staff, as well as providing the tools to maximize class time and improve student achievement.

3. What do you like about earning your degree 100% online?
What I enjoyed most about the online format is that it enabled me to use my time in the most effective manner and allowed me to work it into my schedule, not the other way around.

4. How does this degree compare with other higher education programs you have studied?
I have found this degree program to be fabulous. Learning about the science of the brain and having tools to use to differentiate

instruction based on the principles of how the brain functions is undeniably critical to teaching.

5. Would you recommend this program to other teachers?
Absolutely! Anyone I have the opportunity to converse with about the program, I do! I truly am a devotee to what this program offers and how it can help lead you in your professional advances.

6. What would you say to other teachers about the program?
I would tell other teachers that having knowledge and application skills to teach based on how the brain functions is by far one of the most important components to assist student learning. I would also say that the tools gained are critical to improving teams, fostering teacher development, and creating a culture of leadership that surrounds itself with using the strengths and talents of the group to improve the overall school setting.

7. What would you say to an administrator about the program?
Everyone needs to know how this program facilitates teacher leadership and how it facilitates the Administrative Team. I would tell the Administrative Team that the opportunity for learning best practices in leadership takes place here with BrainSMART. It is an undeniably superb opportunity for professional growth, for both teacher leaders and the administration that supports them.

8. What would you say to parents?
Parents should know that the BrainSMART principles can literally skyrocket student performance and achievement. When you understand how the brain of a child works and the science of what's inside that brain, you are able to create programs of instruction that cater to those needs.

9. What have you enjoyed the most about the content?
I learned so much about the leadership facet of education. Yes, I earned my M.Ed. in Educational Leadership, but earning my Ed.S. in Leadership at Nova taught me cutting-edge skills to be a productive, effective leader—skills that are necessary to promote and support my teachers and other colleagues.

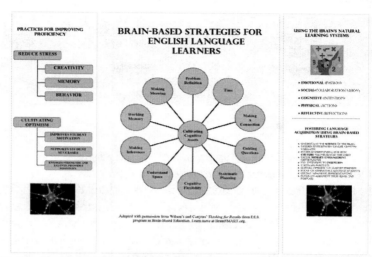

Heather Toner created this poster presentation based on BrainSMART principles for the 2008 Georgia TESOL (Teachers of English to Speakers of Other Languages) convention.

Shirley Ann Carey
Earned: NSU Ed.S. in BrainSMART Teaching
"Our district is heavy into differentiated instruction, and to go through the curriculum in instructional leadership helped me to prepare teachers to differentiate in their classrooms."

1. What grade level do you teach, how long have you been teaching, and what is the name of your school?
I am an instructional coach for teachers grades K through five. I earned an Educational Specialist degree in Instructional Leadership through Nova Southeastern University's BrainSMART program. I have been teaching for 13 years and currently teach in Bibb County Public School District in Georgia.

2. Has the content been useful to you in your work as a classroom teacher?
Yes, as an instructional coach. Our district is heavy into differentiated instruction, and to go through the curriculum in instructional leadership helped me to prepare teachers to differentiate in their classrooms. An instructional coach supports teachers with new initiatives, like a job-embedded staff development. Instead of sending multiple teachers to a workshop, we go to the workshop, then come back and teach it to colleagues. Learning retention and other BrainSMART strategies helps me go into classroom and get the children's attention, because it is so interactive. It is a great way to start and end a lesson. I constantly use the 60 strategies. The "YES" strategy is one of my favorites. I tell the children to talk to another child about how you're going to do well, and they raise their hands and say "yes." They raise their hands over their heads and bring them down and put their thumb inside their fist and say "yes!" It makes them feel they've achieved something, builds their confidence level. It gets them energized, being able to get them up and move.

I try to tap into each of the five learning systems. Learning that the brain likes patterns informs my teaching, such as an increased use of alliteration or categorization to help kids retain the concept. I didn't realize how important the reflective system is. Even though we don't take much time to do it in the school setting, I had students do a lot of reflecting and self-assessment, and only through these graduate studies did I realize how important it is to let these children reflect.

It is so important to have an intact emotional system prior to engaging their cognitive system. My husband and I went through this together and we were both able to apply that in our classrooms. My husband teaches social studies in high school. He also earned the Educational Specialist degree. First, I build a relationship with the kids. They don't care how much you know until they know how much you care. We try to help them feel successful.

3. What do you like about earning your degree 100% online?
It was wonderful. The only drawback was that both of our computers were not networked and we had to get another Internet service. I like 100% online because I didn't have to go out and waste time with a commute and parking. I met students with similar goals and experiences that I shared and did so much more efficiently. I have a younger son and I didn't have to worry about arranging care for him in the evening, especially with both of us being in class. This allowed both my husband and I to do this, and otherwise we would not have been able to do so. The last two quarters the teachers knew we were taking three classes, and they would coordinate how we were going to chat. The instructors worked out our chats for maximum efficiency.

4. How does this degree compare with other higher education programs you have studied?

When I got my master's, I had to drive 30 miles to the school, one way. By the time I got home, I was usually too exhausted to get into my coursework and reading. With this program, I have time to reflect on the concepts and work on my homework. The quality of the information was very, very good. Instructors were helpful and responsive. I had not been in a classroom setting in ten years.

> "When I got my master's [at another university], I had to drive 30 miles to the school, one way. By the time I got home, I was usually too exhausted to get into my coursework and reading. With this program, I have time to reflect on the concepts and work on my homework. The quality of the information was very, very good. Instructors were helpful and responsive."
> —Shirley Ann Carey

5. Would you recommend this program to other teachers?

I really would. In fact, a lot of people look my way and say, "That's your program." It is stuff you can use in the classroom. I would certainly recommend it. It helps as far as being aware of different leadership styles. I got insight into my principal's leadership style. I didn't know his style actually had been given a name in the literature. It helped me professionally and personally. Of course, getting that extra degree, you do get an increase in pay.

6. What would you say to other teachers about the program?
If you're interested in growing professionally and personally, it's a great program. If you're interested in boosting your students' interest and energy, this is excellent information to use in your classroom and personal life.

7. What would you say to an administrator about the program?
Administrators could definitely benefit from the many leadership courses in the program. I would encourage them to push their teachers in this direction because we work with the brain every day, and that's where it all starts.

8. What would you say to parents?
As part of the program, we did a component on getting parents involved. It considers every stakeholder. I would say to parents

this program supports teachers using things like graphic organizers and things that make learning fun and helps with patterns, which is how the brain retains information. This program encourages teachers to use patterns so the brain can retain and recall more information faster.

9. What have you enjoyed the most about the content?
The five learning systems were my favorite. Getting that depth of information about those learning systems and how as a teacher I need to tap into all of them. I try my best to tap into all of them when working with students. When I'm modeling, I might stay in a teacher's classroom for up to two weeks and in that regard I am working directly with the students.

10. Did you have a friend or colleague who took the program? What did they say about the program?
They thought it was great. One has gone on to get her doctoral degree, and she also found the program very convenient. I remember her saying that this has helped her teaching, and she extensively uses a lot of the 60 strategies for boosting test scores. I have modeled these techniques in so many of my peers' classrooms. I feel I have had a real impact in my school.

Ellen Hooper
Earned: NSU Ed.S. in BrainSMART Teaching
"The content of this program has *absolutely* changed the way I teach. It has helped me to recognize what works and what doesn't and how to better excite the children about their music. I love what I do."

1. What grade level do you teach, how long have you been teaching, and what is the name of your school?
I teach strings and orchestra to children in grades three through five. Previously I taught K through fifth grade and have been teaching for 18 years. I currently teach at Bloomingdale Fine and Performing Arts, a magnet school in the Chatham Public School district in Chatham County, Georgia. I earned an Ed.S, with a concentration in BrainSMART.

Ellen and Dewey Hooper, with daughter Julia

2. Has the content been useful to you in your work as a classroom teacher?
The content of this program has absolutely changed the way I teach. It has helped me to recognize what works and what doesn't and how to better excite the children about their music. I love what I do.

3. What do you like about earning your degree 100% online?
It is so convenient to have the luxury to earn a graduate degree from the comfort of one's own home without having to waste precious time on the road commuting to a traditional campus.

4. How does this degree compare with other higher education programs you have studied?
It is peerless in that it allows students to take on this additional work without major disruptions to one's personal life. The quality of instruction and material has been absolutely on par with what one thinks of in a traditional on-campus setting. It is an authentic, rigorous program that has structured itself for busy professionals with considerable work and personal demands.

5. Would you recommend this program to other teachers?
I would strongly recommend this program to other teachers. If you are interested in how the brain works and would like to participate

in a stimulating program that has been organized to fit into today's busy schedules without compromising on the quality of instruction, look into BrainSMART programs at Nova Southeastern University.

6. What would you say to other teachers about the program?
I have recruited peers and family members to these degree programs because the educational techniques I have learned just plain work. It makes me proud to know that I personally help children achieve something that they may have otherwise struggled with. I can do that because I have a great set of tools to help them learn.

> "BrainSMART helps train teachers to not only teach better, but it improves the dynamic among colleagues because everyone is so excited to get a new 'tool kit' they can put to use immediately in the classroom with immediate results. There's a new spark of enthusiasm in everyone from students to teachers."
> —Ellen Hooper

7. What would you say to an administrator about the program?
BrainSMART helps train teachers to not only teach better, but it improves the dynamic among colleagues because everyone is so excited to get a new "tool kit" they can put to use immediately in the classroom with immediate results. There's a new spark of enthusiasm in everyone from students to teachers.

8. What would you say to parents?
Parents should know that BrainSMART teachers truly have the edge when it comes to recognizing what a child needs to learn and how to deliver instruction tailored to a child's particular needs.

9. What have you enjoyed the most about the content?
I specifically benefited from the focus on teacher leadership in the Ed.S. program. I learned how to lead other teachers, and so many creative offshoots came as a result of what I have learned from my graduate studies in this program. It helped me create my own parent workshop, a one-day session for parents of children learning string instruments, a sort-of one-day primer in how to help your

child excel in strings. Parent feedback and enthusiasm has been tremendous, and I get a kick out of seeing the parents get "hooked" and really involved.

10. Did you have a friend or colleague who took the program? What did they say about the program?
I have encouraged some in our family to enroll in a BrainSMART program and a few have. My husband's parents were not able to go to college, but every one of their four children are now teachers. What a powerful tribute to their ability to stimulate their children's sense of discovery, connection, and love of education.

Barbara Peck
Earned: NSU Ed.S. in BrainSMART Teaching
Registered in Brain-Based Leading Minor in the Ed.D.
"When I took the class with best practices and leadership, when I had to get some of my colleagues to participate in the different activities in the leadership book, that was fun. … Being able to share my expertise with my colleagues, they learned from me, used some of the tips in their own classrooms."

1. What grade level do you teach, how long have you been teaching, and what is the name of your school?
I am a diagnostician, with 13 years experience teaching special education. I am certified to teach all ages but for the last six years have worked only with elementary students and focused on learning disabled children. I teach in Georgia's Bibb County Public School system. After earning the Ed.S., I am enrolled in the doctoral program, Instructional Leadership with a minor in BrainSMART.

2. Has the content been useful to you in your work as a classroom teacher?
It has allowed me to discover the different ways children learn and to share that expertise with other teachers. In one of the classes, we got a chance to separate the boys and girls for observation. We found the separation allowed boys to stop worrying about what the girls thought of them. We learned more about the students' personal interests and integrated those into the curriculum whenever possible, to incredible effect. Having this as a "hook" boosted the children's motivation and energy level, and they actually worked harder.

For language arts/literature class, we used a sports theme because the kids were interested in sports. We found sports-oriented books and used subject-verb-pronouns all centered on a theme of sports. The boys couldn't wait to get into the class. They would say, "The girls aren't coming to class, are they? That's good." Since I was so optimistic about trying it, the other teacher working with me didn't mind and supported it, and the professional support of my colleague added even more to our energy level. It was fun to go into work and watch these kids blossom. (We know that the mind of each individual child is different, and that it can be helpful to consider group differences as well. Although it is important to remember that group differences are not as great as the individual differences among boys and girls.)

3. *What do you like about earning your degree 100% online?*
I appreciated the support, availability, and immediate feedback the instructors provided. A few instructors even gave me their telephone number so I could follow up with them if necessary. I like to chat online with fellow students. They shared tips that I could use my classes.

4. *How does this degree compare with other higher education programs you have studied?*
First, the BrainSMART program was more affordable than some of the other programs I looked into. My classes—the cohort I was in—were smaller classes. I knew exactly what my instructors expected me to do. It was not easy work, and I had to perform to earn the degree, but the requirements were always clearly articulated, support was provided, and that's all one can ask for. It helped me develop personal discipline.

5. *Would you recommend this program to other teachers?*
How's this for an endorsement: I have recruited about 15 people who decided to enroll and are earning NSU degrees on brain-based teaching.

6. *What would you say to other teachers about the program?*
It will help you understand your students and their brains. I am helping to develop a whole classroom of lifelong, enthusiastic learners. It's a very powerful and exciting place to be, professionally.

7. *What would you say to an administrator about the program?*

I did share this with our administrator when I was teaching. Learning about the individual and gender differences allows you to differentiate the instruction and that helps them learn differently. You tap into their learning strengths and know how to help them pick up the content.

8. What would you say to parents?

You have a really special teacher who is interested in not only your child but also their brain and what is going on inside their brain. That will help with your child's learning, and parents can count on that helping their child achieve more educationally. I am here to help your child be successful.

9. What have you enjoyed the most about the content?

When I took the class with best practices and leadership, when I had to get some of my colleagues to participate in the different activities in the leadership book, that was fun. We enjoyed that. Being able to share my expertise with my colleagues, they learned from me, used some of the tips in their own classrooms. The content helps me feel more competent and a sense of achievement.

> "Many friends and colleagues have taken the program and have been enjoying it. One friend last week said it has been fun and a great learning experience and has helped her increase her self-awareness."
> —Barbara Peck

10. Did you have a friend or colleague who took the program? What did they say about the program?

Many friends and colleagues have taken the program and have been enjoying it. One friend last week said it has been fun and a great learning experience and has helped her increase her self-awareness. Many have commented about how empowering it has been to tap into their personal strengths and interject those into the classroom setting in a positive way. Optimism has been very helpful!

I used one tip this summer in summer school when, for the last paper, we had to pick one tip out and use it in the classroom. It was successful and I remember, specifically, one memorable child. Then, when Dr. Donna came and taught us a strategy for remembering important healthy high energy foods for peak performance, one of the teachers taught it to their students as a memory strategy. The same teacher started bringing in high protein snacks for the students, and they know that it help their brains to learn. It boosted their self-esteem, too.

Dr. Wilson with Barbara Peck, a diagnostician with Bibb County Public Schools, Georgia

In the class where I was working, we noticed a change in the boys' academic scores; they were more positive and eager to learn. A couple of boys improved their test scores. Some of the boys had previously had behavior problems, and those issues became less significant and distracting in the classroom.

I think it's a good program and a lot of fun, too. Learning about what's going on in the kids' brains has always been interesting to me, but to see how it works and how to teach to it, through different learning styles, means a lot in the classroom and means a lot to the kids. You have successful learners. One day I'm going to teach one of those BrainSMART classes. I already told Dr. Donna I want to teach in the program.

Kim Poore

Earned: NSU M.S. and Ed.S. in BrainSMART Teaching

"The administration sends regular education kids to me with challenges, and this just *works*. I think this program ought to be mandated for new teachers."

1. What grade level to you teach, how long have you been teaching what is the name of your school?

I've been teaching eleven years, eight of them in a self-contained class for behaviorally and emotionally disordered children K through fifth grade. I teach in South Carolina's Lancaster County Public School district. Our school is a Title I school, with a diverse population of African-American, Caucasian and Hispanic children. I have a Master's degree with a concentration in BrainSMART and will soon start the Educational Specialist program.

2. Has the content been useful to you in your work as a classroom teacher?

Definitely, yes. I was able to take what I learned in just one lesson and use it in my class the next day. I love using 10 pegs, and the teaching strategies like snowballs where we would ball up paper and write a test review question, throw it out to the kids, they open the paper wad, read it, respond, and throw it back to the teacher. It is a fresh and effective way to reach these kids.

> "Our entire school does BrainObics every morning with my special ed class leading over closed-circuit TV. It awakens the kids' brains for a day of learning."
> —Kim Poore

Our entire school does BrainObics every morning with my special ed class leading over closed-circuit TV. It awakens the kids' brains for a day of learning. Our special ed class created a character called Nancy Neuron who helps them understand how to rewire the brain and teaches them very advanced concepts of brain architecture and functioning like brain synapses. These are children who are typically very hard to handle, and this sharing has really transformed my classroom and helped them as individuals.

I've been exposed to a lot of workshop material and the theory of the day when it comes to educational theory and practice. I've done a tough kids toolbox and other things for behaviorally challenged kids, and I've never found anything that works like this. The administration sends regular education kids to me with challenges, and this just *works*. I think this program ought to be mandated for new teachers. It is that important to your sanity as a teacher, you shed the battles with the help of these powerful tools. It becomes a joy again to teach these kids. And originally that is why I got into BrainSMART. I had pulled the last rabbit out of the hat. But this program really inspired me and gave me a renewed joy for teaching again. I had been completely burned out.

3. What do you like about earning your degree 100% online?
Teaching special education takes a lot out of me. I do a lot of after-school work, and also teach homebound students and am very busy during the day and up to the evening. Plus, I have my own family. Going to a physical campus was impossible for me. The ability to talk to other teachers and administrators gave me a more global classroom, I was able to share thoughts and strategies with a much broader cohort rather than just a handful of people who happened to sign up for the class in my small town. Interacting with professionals from other states gave me a broader picture of what education was in other regions of the country. The online forums were eye-openers and very interesting to do. You don't get that kind of interaction in a small-town campus classroom.

> "I can't imagine walking into the classroom without the knowledge and strategies that I've learned. It makes my teaching and learning experience more rewarding."
> —Kim Poore

4. How does this degree compare with other higher education programs you have studied?
I have done online classes at Liberty University and a couple through Converse College, and that was all more of a philosophy-driven type of study. It was reading and regurgitate the answers. It didn't give the opportunity to expand one's own thinking, critical thinking or expansion of creativity. I think the requirement of writing skills, really tuning up writing was great because we are required to write at the graduate level. One professor would specifically pick at the grammar. Many think the curriculum might be mickey-mouse because it is online or that it is more akin to buying the credits. It is not. This program holds us accountable. It is so practical and it is required to implement these strategies in

the classroom and report back results. There's nothing like real, live, hands-on experience and this program requires that.

5. Would you recommend this program to other teachers?
Oh, definitely and I have. I talk it up quite a bit. Right now I am working to try and get more awareness of BrainSMART in the Charlotte-Mecklenburg area and will try to promote it for the good of the students and teachers.

6. What would you say to other teachers about the program?
I can't imagine walking into the classroom without the knowledge and strategies that I've learned. It makes my teaching and learning experience more rewarding. They should give this a try.

I decided to try to do my national boards at the same time and what I learned in BrainSMART so closely paralleled the national board standards that I passed easily. I attribute it to working the BrainSMART program simultaneously. I think this is a wonderful thing to do at the same time as trying for the national board.

7. What would you say to an administrator about the program?
I talk to my own administrator quite a bit, and she's very interested in brain-based strategies. I'm going to do a professional development before school begins, this is something for every teacher, novice or seasoned. It will revitalize you, give you energy and encouragement, but you will see immediate results for your students. It is so positive that it will give even a tired teacher energy and joy as they see their students gaining academically and socially from this new way of learning. And I can guarantee test scores will rise. I've seen it with my special ed classes, and I know they will see it with on-level students if my challenged students are performing this well.

8. What would you say to parents?
I would tell them it is important that we all learn how the brain learns so we can all be better equipped to teach. Every brain is capable of learning, but I have seen even my most limited students with measured IQs in the 70s make considerable gains using

BrainSMART strategies. Parents would really benefit from learning these techniques to supplement the learning in the home. It's not so much what curriculum we're using, it's how we get through to these children and this program meets the individual learning style needs for a whole classroom full of children. We are bound to hit on something one of the kids needs when we are focusing and touching on all the learning styles.

9. What have you enjoyed the most about the content?
The knowledge I have gained, there were times I felt I was not doing a good job as a teacher because I didn't have the tools I needed. I haven't arrived, but I have come a long way in this program and it has give me drive to continue to learn about the brain, how it learns, gender differences, and I am a better teacher for the whole child than I used to be. It made me realize I really am a good teacher but needed more tools to reach my teaching potential.

10. Did you have a friend or colleague who took the program? What did they say about the program?
One of the fourth-grade teachers is going through the program, and at least two or three other teachers in our district are now going through the program. They should be close to finishing their Master's. Everyone I've spoken with loves it and puts it in practice in their classroom. One colleague religiously does the BrainObics and pulls out the toolbox and uses the strategies there. I see a difference in her confidence level and now she's quite confident. The district has named me as a mentor special education teacher for others to come observe my classroom. I know this works.

Brooke Bugg

Working toward Ed.S. degree; planned graduation
December 2009

"You're actually learning what you can implement immediately in
your classroom. I also love being able to collaborate with the other
educators. It's distance learning, but with the weekly chat, I feel
more connected with these people even though we may not have
met face to face..."

*1. What grade level do you teach, how long have you been
teaching, and what is the name of your school?*
I teach kindergarten. This is my 12th year teaching. I teach at W.C.
Britt Elementary in Snellville, Georgia.

*2. Has the BrainSMART content been useful to you in your work as
a classroom teacher?*
Yes, even though I'm not entirely done with the program yet, I've
learned a lot of research-based strategies about how the brain
learns best and how to implement those strategies, even in
kindergarten. My colleagues are excited about what I'm doing, and
they always want to know the things I've learned. All students
have the ability to learn as long as they're taught the correct
strategy. I've learned how to create a positive state among my
students, how to make activities more meaningful, how to boost
their attention, how to help with retention, and how to help transfer
what they've learned into their personal lives, not just school.

3. What did you like about earning your degree 100% online?
I love the fact that I don't have to put my family on the back
burner to get my degree. I obviously have to learn to be creative
with my scheduling to still be able to do things with my children. I
have three girls, ages 8, 6, and 2, so life is busy. I commute 28
miles one way to work so I'm on the road almost 60 miles a day. I
love being able to be in my pajamas sitting at home helping my
kids with their homework and get them to bed before turning to the

program—and being able to do all that from the comfort of my home.

It's wonderful because if I actually have to go somewhere on the weekend, all I need is my Internet connection, my flash drive, and my laptop, and it's great having a portable atmosphere. You can be at home, but if you know you have to be somewhere else, you can plan accordingly and still carry on. It's wonderful knowing I can do a valuable program that Nova has without having to live in Florida. The technology and all it's created are great.

4. How does this degree compare with other higher education programs you have studied?
This degree is more hands on and allows you to apply what you've learned, and I really love that. Even when I obtained my master's, I did a literacy program online to help with literacy-based skills. It was okay, but a lot of it was not geared toward kindergartners. But this program seems to be applicable to whatever grade level you're doing, and you can also apply it to your personal life. I love it. It's not simply regurgitated facts like some others that I've done. You're actually learning what you can implement immediately in your classroom. I also love being able to collaborate with the other educators. It's distance learning, but with the weekly chat, I feel more connected with these people even though we may not have met face to face as I have in the past with classes where you actually go and sit with the professor and meet the people. It's really great. I really love that side of the program.

5. Would you recommend this program to other teachers?
Yes. Actually Donna Wilson said that I win the award for getting the most people in the program before I began. I've done three BrainSMART sessions, and I'm hosting two more in March at local public libraries. Whenever we can't get it booked at my school, I just do things in the community. My youngest child was barely 1 when I started researching the program. I knew it was something I was very interested in, but I just had to wait for the right time. My husband and I already had a cruise planned for that summer, and we had tons of things going on. That's why I started

in October. I've probably gotten 50 to 75 people in the program before I even started. I'll be excited in March when I do the session because I'll be able to truly share what the program has done for me and be able to share some of the content and strategies, whereas before I just shared my enthusiasm about what was yet to come.

6. What do you say about this program to other teachers?

I just let them know that it's research-based strategies, things to help their students achieve, to help improve optimism among their students, and things that are just going to support the brain and learning. A lot of this is new research, but I let them know the program has been around for 10 years. I explain to them that it originally started in Florida as staff development programs and in-services, and it became so popular that teachers wanted a degree program out of it. When I heard that and heard other educators talking about it, I really thought it was something for me. I knew that I wanted to move forward with my teacher/leader role, but I wanted to stay in the classroom and still be right there to try out all the things I was learning. They see how enthusiastic and optimistic I am about it, and they're curious and want to know how it can help them, too, in their personal lives and with their students. They get really excited about it, wanting to hear about the latest research so they can try it out with their students.

> "It's amazing how much improvement I've seen in my 5- and 6-year-olds in just the five months that I've been trying the activities. They get excited. They know that I'm going to school, too. They always ask, "What did your teacher say? How was your homework?" They think it's funny that I go to school at night, and they want to know what they can do."
> —Brooke Bugg

It's amazing how much improvement I've seen in my 5- and 6-year-olds in just the five months that I've been trying the activities. They get excited. They know that I'm going to school, too. They always ask, "What did your teacher say? How was your homework?" They think it's funny that I go to school at night, and they want to know what they can do. With kindergartners, they're always active. You have to be very creative and have your bag of tricks ready. Always be ready for the next thing because they are really enthusiastic and always curious about learning, so it's very easy implementing new strategies with that age group. All the teachers have been very supportive, and they see my e-mails when I tell them about the upcoming sessions. We have professional learning days throughout the school year. We can sign up to be learning facilitators so I'm thinking about doing that in the spring. Then, I can actually share some of the BrainSMART strategies that I've learned and give my colleagues some things they can start doing right away, regardless of what grade level they teach. The other teachers are excited about that.

7. What would you say to an administrator about the program?
I'd let them know that learning the BrainSMART strategies and participating in the program would allow them to find out ways to boost student achievement, promote optimistic thinking, and share their leadership responsibilities so they don't feel they have to pull the whole weight of the school. This is what I've just learned in my latest class: It would help them learn to how to create a strength-based organization where all members are learning that they're valued. They're seen as an asset. Everyone feels important. It's not the same people always doing everything. They and their staff would learn how to identify their talents and learn how to move forward in their role as teacher/leaders or administrators, to use their strengths to benefit the common goal of the school. It would just be so important for them to learn about that because there's always going to be some resistance against change and school reform, but this way they would be able to see it as a joint effort and not feel the burden of doing it all themselves. Everyone would be buying into the same mission and goal.

8. What would you say to a parent?
I've actually told some of the parents about ways that they can do different activities at home to help their children. For example, to increase metacognition, we've been using different math exemplars to help strengthen critical and problem-solving abilities. It's just different things they can do at home because I keep

explaining to parents that if they help their children learn to think more metacognitively, they'll be able to transfer that into their school success and into their personal lives. I've been giving them tips on simple things that are free, activities that they can do at home to help their kids be better students. When they feel like they're partners in education with their children, they get excited, and they want to be a part of what their children are doing. Especially in kindergarten, they're usually pretty excited about the diversity and the experience of school. They want to do whatever they can to help their children get ahead. I learned a lot about parallel leadership in the last class. We're learning about how you can evolve a community using parents and everyone working together for a common goal. I'm just trying to share as many quick and easy free activities parents can do at home and reiterate and reinforce what we've been doing at school. A lot of times they'll ask what they can do in the summer to help their children retain what we've done at school and keep them excited about learning. I make homework calendars and I put in suggestions, and I'm even thinking about making a packet this summer suggesting more of the brain-based strategies they can do at home. They really want to know, and they get excited about getting involved in their children's learning. I just let them know that you can tailor the learning to each child's individual needs by utilizing what I'm learning.

9. What have you enjoyed most about the content?
I have enjoyed the research aspect of it. I'm actually learning new things, not just the same old things I learned in undergraduate school. I'm learning how I can take it and apply it right then and there. The instructional strategies are just so useful, whether you're in special ed or regular ed, elementary or high school, there's always a way to adapt it to fit your classroom setting. I've even tried out some of the things with my 8-year-old and 6-year-old at home. It's not something you'll throw away or read about and forget. It's going to be applicable things you can do in your life and in your classroom setting.

10. Did you have a friend or colleague who took the program? What did they say about it?

I kept trying and trying to get a few other people to come on board with me, but it just wasn't the right time for them. I do have a guidance counselor at my school who just started. We haven't been consistently in the same sections of classes, but we do look to one another for support. I also have a friend who teaches in a school seven miles from me—Mary Ann Zudekoff, a special ed teacher at Norton Elementary—who has been in all of the courses that I've been in. We've been a wonderful support system for each other because if we ever want to clarify what we're doing, we can really talk about it and not feel like we're out there all alone. She's a special ed teacher so it's nice hearing a different take on how she can use it with her fourth and fifth graders. I'm regular ed in kindergarten, so we're at different ends of the spectrum. It's nice hearing her perspective and take on things. She feels the same way about me. It's great having even just that one person. We stay connected and we motivate one another. When one of us is feeling down, the other helps with that optimistic thinking. We just help each other think positive and know that we're going to make it through this.

I will tell you it is challenging at times, but to me, it wouldn't be a good learning experience if it were easy. We're learning so much and we're in this together. We're excited that we're really being able to invest time and money in things that are really going to help us and not just help with the pay raise.

Gina Brinkley

Earned: NSU Ed.S. in BrainSMART
Teaching

"Of all the degrees—I have a total of 8½ years of college—this program I completed in 14 months in the convenience of my home, and I can honestly say that I learned more in that 14 months than in the other 7 years of college combined. Way more."

Inspiring Others with the Power of Brain-Based Learning

Gina Brinkley's teaching career has been sidetracked— temporarily, she hopes—by health problems, but she continues to put the BrainSMART strategies to work with young learners and to inspire other teaching professionals with the power of brain-based learning.

The former sixth-grade teacher earned her Ed.S. degree through NSU in March 2007. The following October, Brinkley was forced to go on permanent disability due to health setbacks caused by multiple sclerosis (she was diagnosed in 1999) and a hospital-acquired, antibiotic-resistant staph infection. "I felt like I had lost my identity," she says. "I love teaching, and the BrainSMART program was exactly what I needed. I kept all my books and materials right in my classroom. You should see them—worn from reading over and over, with tabbed pages."

Brinkley moved back home with her parents, and her 10-year-old son, Ashton, now attends the same school his mother went to as a child. Brinkley soon began volunteering in his classroom and found herself "automatically" using BrainSMART strategies when interacting with the children there.

She recalls working with one child in particular—a struggling student who had an especially hard time with math. "I identified his learning style and determined his hemispheric dominance and ran with it," she says.

Within a few days, the boy's astonished math teacher sought out Brinkley to share this story: Every morning, the math teacher put five division problems on the board and typically asked her most academically talented children to step up in front of class to solve them. One morning—after just two group sessions working with Brinkley—the formerly struggling student volunteered to come to the board to solve a problem.

Brinkley began sharing BrainSMART strategies with the teachers and paraprofessionals in her hometown grade school—ideas for teaching cognitive assets, for supporting recall and retention, and for encouraging active learning with movement and praise in the form of "high fives." The principal stopped by a few times to talk with her about the program and how she'd used it both in her teaching and classroom volunteer work.

"The teachers were very interested as they saw the kids get really involved in learning," she says. "Using those strategies made such a difference, it was amazing."

Brinkley was asked to do a staff presentation on BrainSMART. She brought her well-worn books and videos from the degree program, discussed the benefits of distance learning, and even used "many BrainSMART techniques on them."

Gina Brinkley with her Ed.S. diploma

"I'm excited to see that they are excited about furthering their education, not just for the pay increase, but to gain knowledge and insight into the many benefits this program has for teachers," she adds.

Brinkley speaks enthusiastically not only about the practical advantages of the online degree program but also about its "structure and consistency" and the benefits of learning with a geographically diverse group of teachers sharing their experiences from all over the United States. She has plenty of points of comparison. Brinkley earned a bachelor's degree in criminal justice and sociology and previously worked as a juvenile justice officer before becoming a teacher. She earned her master's degree at Georgia Southern University, which entailed a 1½-hour, one-way drive from her home after a full day on the job.

"I'm so glad I discovered the NSU Ed.S. program," Brinkley says. "Of all the degrees—I have a total of 8½ years of college—this program I completed in 14 months in the convenience of my home, and I can honestly say that I learned more in that 14 months than in the other 7 years of college combined. Way more."

What sets BrainSMART apart for Brinkley is the many practical strategies she put to use in her classroom and now as a classroom volunteer. She credits the program with preparing her as an educator "with the tools, strategies, and knowledge of how to use brain-based knowledge to reach my students, to truly reach them and watch the light bulbs going off all over the room—those 'aha' moments that educators love and long for."

Brinkley has encountered many teachers who speak of their frustration and burnout in dealing with the increasing challenges they find in their profession. Most teachers are in the classroom because they love working with children, she notes, and their frustration is very real.

"This program changed the way I view myself as a teacher," she adds simply. "It allowed me to find my strengths and made me confident that I was meeting the needs of my students."

Teacher Leadership and Grants

Some teachers seek to expand their application of what they've learned about the brain, thinking, and instruction by obtaining grants for classroom and school projects. This is the case with Florida teacher Nichole Galinkin.

Grant Helps Teacher Make the Most of BrainSMART Strategies

Florida elementary school teacher Nichole Galinkin was so inspired by the BrainSMART strategies she learned while working toward her master's degree that she applied for and received two grants to build on those ideas in her exceptional student education classroom.

Galinkin, who teaches third through fifth graders, received a $707.50 grant from the Broward Education Foundation CitiBank Success Grant Fund in 2007 for a program she calls "The Power of Positivity (POP) Initiative." Here's how she summarized the program in her grant application:

> The POP Initiative allows elementary students opportunities to discover and apply cognitive thinking skills, which fuels success in school and in life. The skills are explicitly taught in a manner that fosters optimistic thinking, diminishes negativity, and prevents potential dropouts.

"Focusing on strategies to increase optimistic thinking gave my students the boost they needed."
—Florida elementary school teacher Nichole Galinkin

In developing the program, Galinkin came up with a theme for each month incorporating BrainSMART strategies. "Focusing on strategies to increase optimistic thinking gave my students the boost they needed," she notes. "Winning the grant allowed me to buy a lot of motivating materials and fun things to incorporate learning about their brains."

Galinkin received a second $935 grant in 2008 for a program she called PRIDE (for Personal Responsibility in Developing Excellence) Writers. That program focuses on supporting at-risk elementary school student as they apply "essential prerequisite handwriting skills necessary for achievement and success in school."

Incorporating the BrainSMART strategies into her teaching have allowed the 10-year teaching veteran to create "an amazing learning environment" where her students look forward to coming every day.

"A resource room should include activities that are different, fun, safe for risk taking, strategy-based, motivating, and relevant," she says. "I can now say that my room includes all of these elements, and my students are more eager to leave their regular class for their ESE sessions."

Galinkin says she found the resources and books available through the BrainSMART program especially helpful and user friendly. "It's very useful to me to be able to adapt these strategies for use with my students," she says. "But what I've enjoyed most of all is listening to the kids as they remind themselves of a catch phrase or a strategy and hearing them share those strategies with others. It's great to actually see them using the information they're learning."

Nichole Galinkin (third from right, holding the award certificate) receives a grant at the 2008 Citibank Success Fund Grant reception.

Teacher Classroom Research Projects

Research Focuses on Optimism and Learning

One aspect of BrainSMART that impressed sixth-grade teacher Chuck Balogh was its emphasis on the power of positive thinking to increase academic success. He not only put those techniques to work in his classroom, he designed an action research project around optimism and self-reflection.

Balogh did his research with 300 students in the Peoria, Arizona, public school district over almost two full school years. The students in his science and social studies classes came from different economic situations and different backgrounds. A central goal of his research was to increase the positive thinking abilities of learners through self-reflection.

Balogh modeled positive thinking and taught his students the power of optimism. He also encouraged them to write daily in "Happy Books," a technique he adapted based on BrainSMART research that involves writing about emotions, events, and people in students' lives that make them feel happy and optimistic.

Arizona sixth-grade teacher Chuck Balogh

As a result of emphasizing positive thinking to relax and reduce stress about tests, students enjoyed a measurable increase in academic success: Three-fourths or more of sixth graders scored 75 percent or better on the majority of tests taken during the research project.

Balogh credits BrainSMART in helping him to develop an effective teaching approach. The program is "cutting edge, brain-based and proven, and the academic staff is extremely open, helpful and always willing to offer support," he says.

"My research has taken me a lot farther than I ever thought it would," he adds. "It's turned into a passion for me."

Balogh earned his Master's of Science in Education with a Specialization in BrainSMART. His action research paper "Optimism: Can It Increase Academic Success?" is available online through the Social Science Research Network (http://papers.ssrn.com/sol3/papers.cfm?abstract_id=1097682).

Brain-Based Methods Assist Parents

We have found that many teachers and parents alike use our brain-based strategies in their homes with their own families. We hope that as you have shared strategies with your students' parents, you have heard from them how much they have benefited from the insights you shared. Mrs. Brown sent Marcus a thank-you note after he had presented at a regional brain and learning conference in Flint, Michigan, for several years.

Dear Marcus,

Thank you for making a difference in my daughters' lives. I attended a conference in Flint, Michigan several years ago. I attended as a teacher hoping to take away some ideas and information for my students who needed a different approach to learning. I didn't realize at the time what kind of influence the talk you gave would have on my own children.

You spoke of how every night before you went to sleep as a child, your mother had asked you about your favorite part of the day. Then she had asked you what you thought would be a great thing about tomorrow. You also talked about how simple smiles go a long way. You spoke of a positive attitude, nutrition and other behaviors that promote brain function and learning. Allow me to share with you how this information has affected the personalities of my girls.

Something my eight year old daughter, Sydney, said at the breakfast table before school last week made me really understand how connected we all are, regardless of how brief the interaction is. All students in the state of Michigan take a state mandated test (The MEAP). The results of this test are published in the community and used to judge, rank, and evaluate school districts. It is also used to determine whether each school district is making the Adequate Yearly Progress (AYP) required by the controversial policies of No Child Left Behind. While most teachers, principals, parents and students exhibited a great deal of anxiety, Sydney was looking forward to the challenge. She was looking for every advantage that would help her do well. After a good night's sleep, she looked at her plate of food in front of her and said aloud, "Let's see ... proteins first, then fruit, then breads ... right, mommy?" Your advice (I believe you used blueberries...) had become a natural habit at our table.

You may be surprised to know that you also influenced changing diapers in our household. Most new parents dread the waking up every few hours to a crying baby waiting to be nursed or changed. I can assure you that I am no different. I am still trying to make up for lost sleep. However, I would force myself to smile and make eye contact with my girls at three in the morning, as if there were nothing else I would rather be doing.

My daughters also have a great sense of humor, are truly happy and brilliant. Sydney's principal even noticed and asked, "Does she skip everywhere she goes?"

Your philosophy and ideas were really put to the test last year when my six year old daughter, Brianne, was diagnosed with Chiari malformation. When I was told that she would need to have neurosurgery, my heart sank. She was only five years old at the time and didn't realize the seriousness of what was happening to her. Knowing that she would respond based on my reaction, my only option was to put my fears aside and treat it as a medical condition no different than going to the dentist for a filling. I spent many hours in the hospital with her waking up every couple hours crying with pain. Although this was much different than changing diapers at three in the morning, I was able to smile softly at her and tell her that everything was going to be just fine. I would redirect her focus to the painted walls of her room, how it was cool that she got "room service" and her own TV. We made it through a tough year of being cautious (she couldn't even ride her bike or jump rope last summer) before her final MRI and an "all clear" from the neurosurgeon. Yet, the battle for her health and healing is still not over. The amount of fluid that built up in her spinal cord forced her spine to curve over 50 degrees. She will need to wear a corrective brace for scoliosis for a long time. Our positive spirit has allowed us to make wearing her brace a part of everyday life. We can now put it on her with the same sentiment as any routine daily activity such as putting on clothing.

I appreciate the time you took to read my note. Your ideas that I listened to years ago have helped shape the attitudes, personalities and learning process of Sydney and Brianne for a lifetime.

Thank you,
Bridget Brown
Parent and Teacher

P.S. Last night when I asked my 6 year old, Brianne, about what her favorite part about today would be, she said matter-of-factly, "all of it."

Administrators' Stories

Karen Sinclair

Earned: NSU M.S. in BrainSMART Teaching

"The strategies learned in this program teach you as much about your own learning style as it does about the learning styles of your students. This understanding will allow you to model best practices for lifelong learning and leadership for everyone within the learning community."

1. What is your current position, how long have you been in education, and what is the name of your school?

I have been an educator for 31 years. My classroom teaching experience includes pre-K, kindergarten, and second grade public school classroom settings. Since 1991, I have been the Director of First Congregational Church Weekday Preschool and Kindergarten in Winter Park, Florida. Our school offers classes for children ages 2–6 years. We have a total enrollment of 125 children and a teaching faculty of 20.

In the summer of 1997, I attended an Early Childhood Institute for the purpose of recertification. Marcus Conyers facilitated the week-long institute called Brain-Based Teaching and Learning. Since that early BrainSMART introduction, I have attended many conferences and seminars related to brain function, teaching, and learning. Most recently, I completed the BrainSMART Master's degree from Nova Southeastern University.

2. Has the BrainSMART content been useful to you in your work as an administrator?

My colleagues and I have found that the BrainSMART strategies complement the early childhood educational methods and theories that we have studied and draw on to provide for best practices in teaching and learning. We support Jean Piaget's theory that children learn best through play-based experiences. Using cutting-edge research and the latest discoveries in human brain function, the BrainSMART curriculum provides the scientific evidence for *why* children learn best though play. One of our favorite mottos at FCC Preschool comes from a great leader in the field of early childhood education, Bev Bos:

"If it hasn't been in the hand, it can't be in the brain."

3. What did you like about earning your degree 100% online?
Earning my degree online was a great experience, and it was very convenient. I had never used the computer for much more than a word processor and for e-mail. Because of this, I had the immediate experience of novelty, challenge, and purpose! I found that I could do research, complete assignments, and attend online chats in the comfort of my own home. When I was on the go and away from home, it was never a problem to find a place to get online for the chat or to communicate with the instructor. Perhaps the most interesting aspect of the online program was the opportunity to share teaching experiences with professional educators from around the country. Reading the stories and classroom experiences of other teachers was enlightening.

4. How does this degree compare with other higher education programs you have studied?
I earned my first degree at VPI&SU (Virginia Polytechnic Institute and State University) a long time ago (1978). As I think back to compare that experience with the BrainSMART online degree, it seems like comparing apples and oranges. My first degree was in a traditional college setting with very little opportunity for practical application. I remember a children's literature class where we learned the art of storytelling by taking turns pretending to be the teacher or the children. The online master's program requires students to make practical application of new knowledge by using the BrainSMART strategies they are learning within their own classrooms during the course of study.

5. Would you recommend this program to other teachers or administrators?

I would recommend this program to anyone who is interested in teaching, learning and leading.

6. What would you say about this program to teachers or administrators?
I think the most remarkable aspect of this program is that it will teach you more about yourself, your brain/body system, and your learning style than it will about anyone else's. This is important because you will become a much more effective teacher-leader if you understand how your learning style and attitude affect your students. It has been my observation that teachers who are self-actualized are more likely to encourage students to use their natural abilities and curiosity to learn new concepts. The BrainSMART Master's degree provides teachers with a "tool box" of strategies to support differentiated instruction and a library of books and DVDs that will serve as a continual resource for best practices in teaching, leading, and learning.

7. How does the BrainSMART program equip administrators to provide instructional support for teachers?
An administrator's most important role is to build a learning community and to model best practices in education. These responsibilities are completely dependent upon

> "I have used the BrainSMART strategies during faculty meetings to help support a positive learning environment and to encourage a meaningful exchange of ideas among the teachers."
> —Karen Sinclair

continual learning and self-renewal. The BrainSMART program considers the important connection between the teacher/learner and the student/learner. The strategies learned in this program teach you as much about your own learning style as it does about the learning styles of your students. This understanding will allow you to model best practices for lifelong learning and leadership for everyone within the learning community.

The BrainSMART textbooks, DVDs, resource books that complement the curriculum, and Web sites listed to offer additional reading on each subject become a valuable resource library. Administrators can use the BrainSMART resource library to support classroom teachers by providing strategies to differentiate instruction for every type of learner. I have used the BrainSMART strategies during faculty meetings to help support a positive learning environment and to encourage a meaningful exchange of ideas among the teachers.

8. What would you tell parents about the program?
I would tell parents that the BrainSMART program provides the teacher and the student with the scientific knowledge of how their brain/body system is designed to learn best. This understanding supports high academic achievement and inspires students to become lifelong learners.

9. What have you enjoyed most about the content?
The BrainSMART curriculum guides that support each course are full of wonderful strategies for honing teaching skills. They are easy to read and designed to accommodate all learning styles. Together with the DVDs and the resource books that enhance each course, I ended up with a fantastic library to draw on as I continue my learning journey.

What I like most about the content of the program is that the course assignments require practical application of concepts learned, and ask the student to draw on their personal teaching and learning experiences as they gain an understanding of the BrainSMART principles.

10. Did you have a friend or colleague who took the program? What did they say about it?
I have a close friend and colleague who began the master's program when I did (see Cari Rotenberg's story, below). We enjoyed discussions of the courses and assignments and shared ideas with each other as we moved through the BrainSMART courses. My colleague and I agree that this experience was both challenging and enjoyable. We both feel strongly that we have enhanced our own teaching and leading practices.

> ## Cari Rotenberger
> *Earned: NSU M.S. in BrainSMART Teaching*
> "The BrainSMART program definitely gave me tools that I can turn around and say to teachers, 'Here are some strategies that you can use in your classroom.'"

1. What is your position, how long have you been working in education, and what is the name of your school?
I am the Assistant Director at First Congregational Church Weekday Preschool and Kindergarten in Winter Park, Florida. I have been involved in education for 14 years in various capacities, the last four in administration.

2. Has the BrainSMART content been useful to you in your work as an administrator?
Yes, because a lot of times in education in general, but specifically at the early childhood level, we feel we have to defend our position on how we teach young children. Academics are very test driven so we feel we have to defend why we teach children with an emphasis on play at this age. I felt that the BrainSMART content really gave us the tools to be able to give parents concrete reasons for why we do what we do.

3. What did you like about earning your degree 100% online?
I loved the flexibility and convenience. You can work when you have the time to do it. I'm a morning person, so I would always get up early in the morning and work on things before I came to work. Also, about halfway through the program, I gave birth to my first child, my daughter. I was actually able to continue working my way through the program throughout the entire process of adjusting to motherhood because of the format being completely online. That was probably my favorite aspect of it—the flexibility and convenience.

4. How did this degree compare with other education programs you have studied?

I had previously earned an AA degree from Valencia Community College and my undergraduate degree from Rollins College in very traditional classroom settings. Compared to my previous educational experiences, the BrainSMART program is very practical. It's immediately applicable to what you're doing. For instance, my undergraduate degree is in organizational communication. A lot of what I learned was useful, but it was also very theory based. There are lots of differences between what works in theory and what works in practice. This degree in particular—the BrainSMART degree—can be applied immediately in a school setting.

5. What would you say about this program to teachers?

I would absolutely recommend it because not only is it going to help your students learn better, but it's also going to make you a better teacher. You're going to understand how your students learn and how you learn as well.

6. What would you say to an administrator about this program?

I would say, "If you have teachers who are interested in doing this program, any way that you can support them as they're doing it or encouraging them to do it would be great." I would also suggest that administrators take this program because then they could understand a little bit more about the strategies teachers are putting in place in the classroom.

7. How does BrainSMART equip administrators to provide support for teachers?

The BrainSMART program definitely gave me tools that I can turn around and say to teachers, "Here are some strategies that you can use in your classroom." For instance, helping children transition is often something that's very difficult at the early childhood level. I remember specifically working with a teacher to teach the children in her classroom BrainObics so that when she was transitioning between activities and time in the classroom and time outside the classroom, it made those transitions go a little bit smoother.

8. What would you say to parents about the program?

This goes back to how we teach young children. Parents often ask me, "How do you teach pre-reading? How do you teach ABCs? How do you teach math?" Now I feel like what I can say to parents is that this is the science behind what we do and this is why I embarked on this journey of this degree program. Not only did I want the tools, but I also wanted to be able to justify why we teach children the way we do.

9. What have you enjoyed most about the content?
For me, this goes back to theory vs. practice. Everything that we learned is very practical and very easy to apply. There's immediate application of the strategies. The assignments are useful because they force you to apply the knowledge that you're learning and reflect on your learning. I always think that new knowledge is only as good as the extent to which you use it. For example, in each of the courses, we're required to create an artifact. In one of the classes I took all of the learning I had acquired about the anatomy and physiology of the brain, and I revamped our entire Web site for the school so that parents could access a three-dimensional Web site that gave them information about the brain, tools for planning healthy snacks and lunches for their children, and those kinds of things. I think it's very practical. There's that immediate application. You can really take it and use it. You can see how it works in your classroom at your school.

10. Do you have a friend who took the program? If so, what did they say?
Karen Sinclair and I took the program together. She is our director. I think the thing that we both would say is that it was wonderful to have someone in the same school doing the program. It's not face to face in the classroom, so it was nice that Karen and I could get together and talk about things. We could bounce ideas off of one another. We could say, "How are you approaching this assignment? What did you think about this book we read?" I think we would both agree that it's nice to have someone doing the program with you.

Ideas for Next Steps

In this book you have seen how many BrainSMART teacher leaders have used strategies to model effective teaching and to help their colleagues become more effective teachers. In addition, you may find strategies from the following article useful in your work as a teacher leader.

BrainSMART Teacher Leadership
By Marcus Conyers, Co-Founder BrainSMART

"Using new teaching strategies in the classroom may be like a fountain of youth for your brain. As a mentor, helping your colleagues understand this may help get more people excited about changing classroom practice."

While working with many states and districts across the country through the years, I have been thoroughly impressed by the teacher leaders' positive response and full engagement. This engagement represents a professional commitment to continuously improving

Marcus Conyers presenting BrainSMART methods at a conference

student learning. It is apparent in all that you do.

As I travel across the country, I get to meet teacher leaders in almost every state, and one of the most common questions I receive is, "How can I more effectively mentor my colleagues?" With this question in mind, the goal of this article is to support you with research and strategies for effective mentoring. This topic is close to my heart because our goal is to assist every teacher we can to have more ways to reach and teach students, and good mentoring can be an effective way to do this.

The great news is that breakthroughs in brain and cognitive research are indicating some new ways of engaging the adult brain. As always, our focus is on translating this research into practical strategies that can be applied right away. In this article I will focus on a brief outline of current research, school change, and a model for understanding how the adult brain learns and functions.

The BrainSMART Framework for Cognitive Functions

Current research on human brain function suggests that each human being is as unique as a fingerprint. All of us start out with similar brain wiring for basic survival. Then our life experiences and formal education work to create new wiring throughout the brain. The great news is that we can keep positively rewiring our brains throughout our lives so that we can learn to think and communicate even more effectively. The key to this positive rewiring is to have a steady stream of novelty, challenge, practice, and feedback.

When we continuously expose our brains to new challenging activities and keep practicing while getting feedback from colleagues each day, we may wake up with a slightly better brain! We always begin with this great information whenever we conduct professional development in schools because it gives a strong incentive for teachers to learn new teaching strategies that not only increase student

> When we continuously expose our brains to new challenging activities and keep practicing while getting feedback from colleagues each day, we may wake up with a slightly better brain!

learning but also make their own brains smarter. We use the following framework for understanding some key brain functions (of course, each brain area is involved in many other processes):

Back brain: Receives sensory information
Left brain: Focuses on the familiar and repeats existing behaviors
Right brain: Focuses on novelty and generates new ideas
Front brain: Puts new ideas into practice

Current educational leadership literature is clear that the single most important factor in improving school performance is classroom instruction. Therefore, innovative teacher leaders are critical in this mission.

The Change Pyramid

Current research suggests that in most organizations there are four main groups of individuals. At the peak of the pyramid are the innovators. These individuals are most likely to use innovative practices for improving student learning. Next are the early adopters. These individuals are often the most open to adopting new practices once they see them in practice. Next come the majority, who will usually change over time as they observe new ideas being implemented by a larger number of people. The final group is described by researchers as laggards. These folks are usually the very last to change. In short, it is the innovators and early adopters who usually pull schools and other organizations toward positive improvement. For this reason teacher leadership and mentoring are critical. In our work with thousands of educators, we have learned that when it comes to providing mentoring, it is best to begin by focusing time and energy on innovators and early adopters as these individuals are most likely to make positive changes. As these individuals change their practices, the majority are more likely to change over time. It

> In our work with thousands of educators, we have learned that when it comes to providing mentoring, it is best to begin by focusing time and energy on innovators and early adopters as these individuals are most likely to make positive changes.

is usually not a good investment of time and energy to focus on those whom research refers to as laggards.

The BrainSMART Barcode for the Brain

One of the most difficult activities for human beings is to understand other people's points of view and motivation. To aid this understanding we have developed brain-based leadership strategies; in doing so we have found that it is extremely important to create a clear understanding of how different colleagues think, learn, and communicate. Such  understanding is based on what we call the Barcode for the Brain, nicknamed S.T.R.I.P.E.S., which is based on current research in cognitive psychology. As mentioned previously, early life experiences and formal education tend to wire brains in different ways. The great news is that we can keep rewiring our brains throughout our lives if we wish. This model can be used effectively by educational leaders to individualize leadership and mentoring.

Similarities and Differences

The first stripe on the Barcode for the Brain deals with whether people look for similar experiences (i.e., they have great comfort with familiarity) or whether they seek out new and different 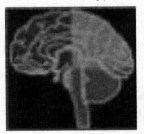 experiences. This barcode is neither good nor bad – it just indicates a cognitive preference. Individuals with a "sameness code" are often extremely comfortable with the familiar and are keen to repeat practices that are familiar to them. They may live in the same town where they grew up – often living on the same street, attending a local college, even going back to teach in the classroom where they were taught as a child. These individuals are often happy to repeat the teaching practices they saw their own teachers use when they were a student. This approach works well if the teaching practices they use are effective with today's students. Additionally, these individuals are often strong at using received information to reinforce existing behaviors.

At the other end of the spectrum are individuals with a "difference code," who seek out novel experiences. They too may stay in the same town where they were born, go to a local college, and return to teach in the same school where they were educated. However, these individuals often seek out new and different ways to teach when they become aware that old teaching practices are not effective with the brains of today's students. As such, people who seek out difference may be more open to innovative ways of teaching. They may also be keen to constantly improve themselves and their brains.

Whether a person prefers similarities or differences is an important element to consider when mentoring. If the person you are mentoring is a Sameness person, it is often good to begin by honoring what they are currently doing and then work on small adjustments that will increase effectiveness over time. If the person you are mentoring is more of a Difference person, you can be open about new and different ways of teaching as this approach will be highly motivating and exciting to this individual.

Toward or Away

Toward or Away is the second stripe in the Barcode for the Brain and refers to one's attitude to life. Some people are moving Toward. This means they tend to have an optimistic outlook and are constantly moving toward goals such as improving student learning, teaching more effectively, or raising student achievement. These individuals are most motivated by a mentor who can help them effectively move toward their goals. In contrast, Away individuals are more motivated by avoiding discomfort, risk, or loss. With Away individuals a good mentoring approach may be to help them see that by adopting new practices, they can avoid problems such as low student performance or disruptive students. Perhaps not surprisingly, if you are a Toward person, it is often difficult to understand individuals who are Away. Again, it takes practice to understand another's point of view. Once you can honor this point of view, you can build a much better relationship.

Reactive or Proactive

This barcode refers to whether people are Reactive or Proactive. Reactive individuals tend to excel if there is an emergency or if there is a clear and present difficulty that needs to be solved today. They are often quick to act and are motivated by immediate problems and opportunities. At the other end of the scale are Proactive individuals; these people are keen to prevent problems before they happen. They tend to have a long-term outlook and often excel in planning activities. Proactive teachers tend to work extremely hard at creating a positive classroom environment as a way to improve student behavior and to develop interesting and engaging instructional practices that increase student learning. Reactive individuals will tend to wait until there is a problem and then work very hard to solve it.

In Time or Through Time

How the human brain processes time can vary significantly from individual to individual. Some people live fully in the moment – we call this living In Time. These individuals are completely engaged in the experience of living minute by minute. At the other end of the extreme are people who are Through Time; they tend to live in a world that is highly structured in terms of time. They excel at the use of time planners and often plan their time very tightly and well. When working with Through Time people, it is important to carefully plan time commitments as this will tend to put them at ease and help them focus their energies appropriately. For people who are In Time, it's important to help them fully engage in the positive experiences of implementing new ideas. Such experiences are very motivating to them.

Procedures or Options

The Procedure or Options barcode refers to whether people prefer to have procedures in their lives or whether they prefer to focus on options. Procedural people are often happiest when there is a clear beginning, middle, and end in whatever task they are doing. Their great strength is that they tend to finish what they begin. For example, Procedural shoppers will go to the store with a list, move at mimicry position from aisle to aisle, have the coupons ready as they check out, and can probably correctly guess the amount of the bill. In stark contrast are Options individuals; these people constantly seek out new ideas and ways to do things. When they shop, it is more like an adventure safari as they seek out products that are new and improved and offer more options and choices. The differences between Procedures and Options individuals should be considered when mentoring colleagues. When mentoring individuals who like procedures, the best method is to go through ideas step by step to provide structure and comfort. Alternatively, for Options individuals it is great to outline the general principles of what can be done and then suggest several different options.

External and Internal

Externally driven individuals tend to be concerned with what others think. They watch what other people do, look for reactions, and determine what course of action is best. For example, when a school is implementing new professional development, External individuals will watch what others do; if they see others getting engaged and involved, then they will follow suit. Such individuals are often good at reading others and are empathetic. On the other end of the scale are individuals who are more Internally driven; these individuals are mission-focused and keen to get results. They are much more influenced by their own individual experiences than by others' opinions. When mentoring these individuals, an effective approach is to let them experience for themselves how well something works. This experience will motivate an Internal individual. In contrast, External individuals might prefer seeing presentations of new teaching strategies as well as the opportunity to see others applying the new strategies.

Specifics and Big Picture

This barcode refers to whether people are more motivated by seeing the Big Picture or by getting the Specifics right. For example, we often help schools develop an improvement plan to share with their community; this task is usually most exciting to Big Picture people who are excited about a larger vision that is motivating and energizing. Specifics-minded individuals are more concerned about ensuring that the specifics are correct and in how the details of such a vision could be implemented.

To summarize, we sincerely hope that as a teacher leader, you are finding current ideas and strategies in your graduate studies you can use as you seek to mentor colleagues. In the video on the Barcode of the Brain, you may also find strategies for reaching different types of learners in the classroom.

Note: This article is based on a keynote presentation titled, *BrainSMART® Mentoring for NBCTs:Research-Based Strategies for Mentoring Colleagues,* which was funded by the Florida National Board for Professional Teaching Standards. Other presentations of Conyers's work in the area of teacher leadership and mentoring have been featured at the national conference for NBPTS, as well as in several large districts within the United States.

Conclusion

It is our intention that you are inspired by "your" stories—that is, the stories and interviews of those who have studied the BrainSMART approach to instruction. Many readers are considering entering these graduate programs, are current students in the programs, or are program graduates.

We hope you have found these stories about the teacher leaders who have inspired us useful. Throughout time the human brain has learned much by listening to stories, reading books, and seeing movies. Most importantly, we hope that through your program and reading these stories, you will be inspired to create your own story as teacher leader, experience for yourself the thrill of seeing your students learn more as their light bulbs switch on, and enjoy seeing that you have had a positive impact on your colleagues. As you do so, if you want to share your story, please contact Karen Bankston. Her address is stories@brainsmart.com. We hope to hear from you!

About the Authors

We now stand at an exciting point in history when we can put research about cognition and the brain into practice so that all students can become smarter.
—Donna Wilson & Marcus Conyers

Donna Wilson and Marcus Conyers are authors of 14 books on the brain, cognition, and learning and co-developers of the graduate programs in brain-based education with Fischler School of Education at Nova Southeastern University. To date, some 1,700 educators from across the United States, Canada, Europe, and Japan have enrolled in these cutting-edge programs. For more than 30 years the team has translated research from the fields of cognitive psychology and brain research into systems and strategies for teaching, leading, and learning. As co-developers of the BrainSMART model, Donna and Marcus have personally shared their practical research-based strategies with more than 125,000 educators across the United States and Canada and in the United Kingdom. Their mission is that by 2020 every child will be learning the cognitive skills they need to thrive in the global, brain-powered 21st century economy. To learn more about the graduate programs, see the short videos and other materials at www.brainsmart.org.